Dedication

I dedicate this book to everyone who has had
an impact on me whether they knew it or not.
A special dedication to my Grandma,
Melinda Williams, who would have been so
proud of her grandboy. My dear friend,
Gary Curtis, who believed in me when no
one else did. My friend and fellow Hood
Scholar, Herbert Johnson, whose life was
taken in a senseless violence. Dr. Hollins
who encouraged me when I tried so hard to
quit.
Your names will forever live on through me.

◉ ◉ ◉

1

Contents

Part 1: The Boy

Part 2: Principles

Part 3: The Transition

Part 4: Major Keys

Foreword

By Will Cyrus

CEO Cyrus Consulting Group
(@project2profit)

Every individual in the world has a hood scholar defining a moment in their life. If we look at Webster's dictionary, the phrase "Hood" has a derogatory meaning behind it. From those with outside opinions, they would define it as something dangerous. But to those of us who grew up in those conditions, we understand that this hood is what has cultivated us into becoming the men and women we are today. There are a lot of life-long messages that you can learn in this environment.

In fact, it might be one of the best business schools in the world. It is the only place in America where you can learn any skill for free. Kids are learning skills that one would get taking up a psychology degree by the time they turn 12. Some kids are starting their own businesses as early as elementary school. Growing up in the hood might be the best thing that could have happened to some of us inner city kids who have made it out and become successful living citizens. I encourage you to read this book as it challenges the status quo of what it means to be a "Hood Scholar" and how you can defy the odds to become one.

Preface

It's been a long road, and it hasn't been perfect, but I can assure you it has been worth it. When writing this book, I was faced with some of my most difficult trials and tribulations to date. I told God I am trying to live right the best way I know how. I still couldn't seem to understand most of the chaos while I was going through it.

As this book receives its finishing touches, I see now that most of it wasn't for me but to touch a reader going through a rough patch. I have learned some of the most valuable lessons in life while preparing this project. There were many mountain and valley experiences while on the road to become the Hood Scholar.

* * *

Highs and lows along with some out of this world experiences. My goal is to touch one reader and encourage them to be great in their regard. Also, to inform readers that where you are from doesn't have to dictate where you end up in life.

This book will allow readers to realize there are multiple ways to make it out the hood. Similar to a GPS, no matter the route we take, we can all end up at the same destination. Just because you took the toll route and got to the destination earlier doesn't mean I can't meet you there. If one reader is encouraged to chase their dreams because of this project, my goal has been met.

Part 1: The Boy
Chapter 1

Close Call

It was the summer of 2017 and the last summer before I would graduate college in the spring of 2018. The semester before, I had a 1.74 GPA, and I was thinking about dropping out and continuing my current hustle. Graduation was the last thing on my mind. I'm not quite sure how I had found myself in the spot that I was in, but I was there. It was a plethora of events that led to me being in the headspace that I was in. I was down on my luck and almost ready to cash in my ticket on life.

Just a year before, I was thrilled going into the football season because we would be playing Texas A&M on ESPN. However, I had no clue what the next year would

* * *

bring. I imagined myself somewhere preparing to give the NFL my best shot. In less than a year, I was running with a different crowd of people and doing things that I am too ashamed to talk about today. What I can say is that the activities that I was partaking in came with a hefty prison sentence. And by hefty, I mean more years than I had lived on this earth. On this particular day, I had ignored every sign that God had sent to me. I was back home in Florida for my younger sister's graduation. Hard off for money, an associate of mine came to me with a proposition. My credit card was over drafted, and I had less than $20 to my name. He was a witness to a murder in my hometown, the police had made him a suspect, and he was in a deep panic. In the panic, he told me that If I drove him back

* * *

with me to college, he would pay off my credit card and give me $500. Yeah, I know, pretty wise thinking by the hood scholar. He suggested that we get some marijuana for the trip, and I thought it was a bad idea. Thinking with my brilliant mind, I let him talk me into grabbing almost 10 grams for the trip. The trip was 18 hours, so I did need to prepare my mind for it. We were on route to Texas in a red drop top 2017 Volkswagen bug. I made sure that I was doing the speed limit the whole ride. Once we made it to Louisiana and had about three hours to go, we had already smoked all but maybe two grams of the marijuana. I saw a police officer in the next lane, and he began playing games with me. I was so high that I began to play the games also. He slowed down to get behind me, and I started driving slower than he was. I was going almost 5 mph on I-10. My associate panicked because we were so high, and the car was fogged full of smoke. Remembering he was on the run for murder, he insisted me to floor it. I kept calm and wouldn't let him worry too much. I kept calm when the officer came to the car and asked if I had known I was swerving. I know for a fact that I wasn't swerving, but that's a whole different story. He asked if I had been smoking, and I told him no. He didn't check me, so I figured the guy in the passenger seat would eat the weed or put it in his underwear. The officer moved us to the back of the car on the side of the highway. I whispered to my associate, asking where the drugs were, and he said that they were under the seat. I was pissed and just knew

* * *

we were going to jail. He was so nervous about the murder that he thought he was about to go to jail forever.

He convinced me to tell the officer it was my weed because the officer was picking at him. The officer asked me where we were going, and I told him I was taking my associate back to watch our summer football practice at the college. He googled me and saw some of my accomplishments. They searched the car in a manner I had never seen before. They checked the hood and even under the car, looking for all the hotspots. I was sort of off the hook when they were searching my suitcase and found my cleats. The officer came back to us and asked why my associate was looking so nervous. He said he hoped we weren't nervous because of the two grams under the seat. He told us they were looking to hit the jackpot, and that this was nothing to worry about. I believed they smoked themselves. I let out a sigh of relief and figured the coast was clear. The officer wanted me to blame the marijuana on my associate so that they could take him into custody. I told the officer they were my drugs, and he poured out the bag on the side of the road. I knew this was nothing but God's grace.

Returning home from Texas last year, the same associate and his cousin went on a police chase in the same town while heading back doing the same thing. It has been over a year, and his cousin is still sitting in that same jail in Louisiana with no bail. This was a sign from God that I had to get my life back together. I knew that If I didn't get my life together where I would be headed. Many of the people who I was hanging with at this

(Starting line up on ESPN in 2016 from Prairie View
A&M Panthers vs. Texas A&M Aggies)

time in my life are either in jail, dead, or
not doing anything with themselves. That's
such a scary thought when you think about
it. Sometimes I wonder why he chose me to
save. I struggle and sometimes feel guilty
when I think of the other people I had been
hanging out with that summer. The fast life
was no joke and I had taken it for granted. I
was just thankful that I was able to get out
when I did and knew I had to make it count.

HARRIS COUNTY, TEXAS
OFFENDER IDENTIFICATION CA

Ham   Jovante
SPN: 02803237
DOB: 10/28/1994
Probation Term:
01/20/2016   to   07/20

Court: 003   County Criminal Court
Offense: THEFT
Cause: 2038324

(Probation offender card from when I was arrested in 2016)

Chapter 2

The Crib

Broward County, Florida. Fort Lauderdale, Florida. Thirty minutes from Miami. Exotic Beaches and beautiful women. Millionaire lifestyles and billionaire dreams, right? Not even close. Murder is the norm, and a college education is almost unheard of. A place where graduating high school could be one's biggest accomplishment, and only a small population have even earned their diploma. But to us, this is normal. Growing up, the goal was to become hood rich.

The fast money capital of the USA. No one dreamed of being a doctor or engineer. This was because we knew no one before us who had done so. Until I reached high school, I hadn't even known anyone who had even been to college. So, it seemed like a rich person's activity to many, especially if it wasn't through sports. Everything I have accomplished so far was by the grace of God. No blueprint or foundation was laid out.

Lately, I have been setting goals that look impossible to attain. Slowly but surely, they are being checked off the list. I once thought that I was the chosen one and couldn't understand my recent success.

After careful consideration, I then began to realize that I'm a minor character playing a big role in my own life. I am being used as a tool for the younger generation. When we look back at all the great people in history, they were the first to do certain things. How can a system fail one it was never made to protect? I could get caught in the hype and brag and boast about my success. But the thing is I'm not worthy of it, and I realized this quite some time ago.

The same way kids dream of becoming the next Michael Irvin is the same way some will dream of becoming the next Jovante Ham. He was the first from Broward County to make it to the Hall of Fame, and we must admit that it is quite an accomplishment. But sad to say, only less than 1% of the kids playing high school football will make it to the NFL. What about the other 99%? They need someone to look up to, someone who looks like them, from the same place that went on to do something great. It all starts with one. We must have faith, and this new generation needs to touch and feel the success. I have been blessed to be in a position where no one has been before me. I'm speaking from the perspective of a young kid out of the projects that has been to college and also to jail. A child with no role model, who became an Aerospace engineer and entrepreneur with two college degrees. One might say you're not the only one from the hood to become an engineer or entrepreneur. But it's so much more than being an engineer and entrepreneur.

I might not be the first, but I can assure you that I am the first from my hood. The first one that will proudly tell the kids that they too can become rich not only by their athletic abilities. By rich, I am not speaking of monetary standards, but a rich spirit and a rich mindset. The mindset will eventually lead to the funding. I will prove that the drug dealers and credit card scammers are not the only ones with money. I will teach that being rich in spirit is much more than becoming hood rich. I will teach how to obtain this mindset. I will let you into the mindset that eventually led me to become the hood scholar.

Chapter 3

Hood Scholar

Hood is defined by the Urban Dictionary as being from the inner city and expressing the essence of urban culture. A scholar is defined by Webster's Dictionary as a person who is highly educated or has an aptitude for study. A hood scholar is someone who defied the odds despite their surroundings, going above and beyond educating themselves whether it be through school or self-education.

I have a special place in my heart for hood scholars because I know the struggle first hand. When the standard was never set, how could one know their limits? A lot of my classmates were legacy in college, meaning their parents and/or grandparents attended the university. Well, for me, my mom went to the army and completed her associates shortly after, and my dad never graduated high school. It was never a requirement or any pressure that I had to live up to. I would think someone who has two parents that hold college degrees are almost required to go to college. To be honest, if it weren't for football, I probably would have never attended college either. My parents had no college fund for me or anything of that nature. The situation of how I even got to college was very crazy in itself. My senior year in high school, I was the Broward County 5A-8A Player of the Year. Everyone else who received the award went to very big D-1 universities. I knew that if I worked hard and stayed humble, my time would soon come. But around two weeks before signing day, I began to panic. I had to sign

(Signing day 2013 at Dave & Busters in Hollywood, FL on NBC 6)

on national television alongside people
who held offers from Alabama, LSU,
Miami, and many more. My coaches and
family were very confused, and I was too.
Now that I think back, I remember praying
that the Lord give me an offer so that I could
have something to announce on television in
the coming weeks. My dad wanted me to
sign to a junior college, but my pride
wouldn't let me sign to a junior college on

national television. I have a special note that I use to tell myself now that I wish I had known back then.

Sometimes you might not understand what's going on in your life because it doesn't line up with your history, but it lines up with your destiny. I remember crying many nights and wondering what I did wrong. I had amazing film and grades, so I figured last resort I would go to a small D-1 FCS school. A couple of weeks before signing day, one of my former teammates whom I was close with and had already gone to college was home for the holidays. He was in the coach's office and was playing my highlight tape when his coach walked by. The coach asked who I was and what my status with signing was. He immediately contacted me and told me he loved my film. He said he would get back to me but couldn't make any promises because it was so close to signing day. So again, I prayed. It was maybe the hardest I had ever prayed. I can't remember word for word, but I can recall me begging God just to give me this one shot, and I would not mess it up. The coach called me back the next day and said the scholarship was down to this other guy from Houston and me. He told me that we were about even, and he was really pulling for me to get that last scholarship. He said he didn't know how he was going to do it, but he was going to make sure I would be a Prairie View Panther. Despite me having almost a 3.8 GPA at this time, I was planning on being a Criminal Justice major to become a crime scene detective. I was great at math and science but never really liked applying myself and wanted to take the easy way out.

Watch what you pray for because it just may end up coming true, and it may be to the exact circumstances you asked for. The coach called me back two days before signing day and said that they gave the scholarship to the other guy. He informed me that they had a scholarship for me too, but it came with a catch. For the first year until some money cleared up, football would pay for half, and if I wanted the other half paid for, I would have to be an engineering major. This was bad news for me because although I was a hard worker on the field, I never cared for school. Besides, I knew that whatever school I went to, I was going to make it to the NFL anyways. But nonetheless, that was my only offer, and I had heard how much engineering majors made after college and that sounded like a plan. I didn't know the definition of engineering much less what they did. He told me I had to choose a discipline, and I didn't have a clue. I always liked computers growing up, so I went out on a limb and chose computer engineering. I was very skeptical about the decision, but the night before signing day, the wide receivers coach called me and assured me that it was possible to be an engineering major and play football because he had done it. He told me how he knew people in the department and would set me up with good mentors when I got there. With the timing so late, I wasn't even able to visit the school before signing with them. The same friend who showed my highlight and another friend from high school were there, so I went off with what they told me and signed on the dotted line. I took a leap of faith, and it

* * *

ultimately would become one of the single best decisions I had in my entire life. When arriving at school in the summer, I came alone because both of my friends were home for the summer. I met a woman named Dr. Hollins, who made me feel so at home. She was very motherly to me and looked out for me when I knew no one in Texas. The first semester was very hard, and I had talks with her about changing my major. She told me to stick it out and ensured me that I would be okay and that she would set me up with teachers I would be successful with. Suddenly, Dr. Hollins died the next semester at 33 years old. At that moment, I told myself that no matter how tough engineering got, I would never switch my major. It got very tough, but ultimately, I stayed focus. I knew it was God, it had to be God.

* * *

Chapter 4

Gotta' be God

It was early 1994, and my mom had just found out she was pregnant. Just an ordinary day in her life, but it almost changed forever. She was trying to hurry and leave out of an intersection. She began to proceed behind a city bus and was blindsided out of nowhere. She was hit so bad that she didn't even remember what happened. This was 1994, and there were no seatbelt laws. Thank God she was always proactive and very careful because the doctor said that the windshield would've killed her and her baby if she wasn't wearing her seatbelt. Some people believe in coincidences but not me. I took this into account as my first blessing, and it was long before my first breath.

Although being on this earth merely a quarter of a century, I have had my back against the wall countless times. And whether it be me, family, or friend's prayer God is the formula behind the deliverance from these issues. I can go back to as recent as yesterday and as far back as me being an infant when prayer has been the tool behind everything. When I was born, I had trouble using the bathroom. It went from bad to worse when I was diagnosed with Hypospadias. This is a congenital disability where a male's tube that carries urine to the bladder is on the wrong side. It was very rare, but my family took to one thing to get everyone through the situation, and that was prayer. They prayed over me as a child as I had to go through surgery at just five months old.

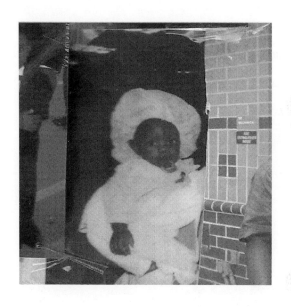

(Me pictured at 5 months old following surgery)

Surgery was successful at first, but then I began to have more complications. They had to go back over the surgery when I was 18 months old, and I have not had a problem since. Although this was one of the first cases were God saved my life, it would most definitely not be the last. Fast forward about 11 years, this was an even more frightful situation. My family is very spiritual, building our backbone on the Lord Jesus Christ.

A young me had it in my heart but had never really had my first real encounter with the Lord until I was about 12 years old. I can remember it like it was yesterday. It was the week before Christmas, and all my cousins were spending the night at our house. I woke up one morning and couldn't walk. I tried to step but fell completely to the ground. I told my mom and family, but everyone thought I was playing. Well, a few days later, they realized that I was telling the truth. When arriving at the hospital, we thought maybe I just had a sprained ankle or something of this degree. After diagnosing me, they quickly realized it was a much serious matter. I had a chipped bone in my ankle for months, and fluid had built up and caused an infection. The doctors said that they would try hard to drain the fluid, but if not, my foot would have to be amputated. This was the first time I can ever remember praying with a purpose.

I constantly prayed all night and day. The pastor from my aunt's church came along with their congregation and prayed over me also. They included me into their prayer lists, and all I remember doing at the hospital was praying. Needless to say, a week after admitting me, all the fluid was gone, and three weeks later, I was back to my normal routine and trying out for my middle school track team. Now thinking back on this situation, losing my foot in middle school would have been tragic for my life. And who's to say that if not for prayer I might have lost a foot and my life would be totally different today.

This last instance is maybe the hardest one I've had to deal with in my adult life. I was finally the starting running back at Prairie View A&M University after waiting three years for my turn. A week before the first game, my advisor informed me that despite having had a 3.0 GPA, I was a credit short of the degree percentage for going into your fourth year. I had taken thermodynamics the summer semester before the season and knew I had to pass it to play. I gave my all, and when final grades came out, I had a D. I had explained the situation to my professor before grades were finalized and felt pretty confident in my performance. So, I went to talk to the professor, and she informed me that my final grade was a 68.7 which round up to a 69. One point away and she didn't look to pass me. She went on to explain how she really didn't care about my situation, and that thermodynamics was the only class she failed in college. I then began to pray. I asked God to please make a way for me to play. I remember shortly after praying and waiting two hours outside her office to speak with her. She said to me that there was nothing she could do and that I should indeed pray about the situation. Hearing this from her encouraged me to pray a little harder. After not giving up, she told me that there was a slim chance that she would change my grade. She said I would have to re-take the final exam and pass it to be awarded a passing grade. The semester had been over about a month now, and thermodynamics was not one of my strong points. Before taking the exam, I prayed some more. I refused to give up on praying because due to previous circumstances, I knew the power of it. To my surprise, I got a lower score than I did the first time. I still chose to pray, even when I felt defeated. She then told me there was no way I could pass the class. I asked God again for any way that He could change my grade. Notice that I said "He" and not she. He was bigger than this situation. Now the first game was two days away.

Something led me to ask to see her grade book, and I just happened to have all of my old exams in my backpack. I wouldn't believe this next thing I'm about to tell you if I wasn't there myself. She had given me a lower grade in her grade book than what I received in the exam. I'm not sure how and why this took place, but I'm a firm believer that God stepped in with his power. This happened just in time for me to get her to sign my grade change form. Now all I had to do was get the form signed by the dean and the vice provost, and I was good. Well, guess what, the dean happened to be out on vacation. I then prayed a little bit harder. I was able to get the form signed by the associate dean and the vice provost the day before the game. I do believe God could have taken care of the situation much quicker, but he wanted me to elevate my prayer life. Praying and being persistent is vital. He can show up and show out. When you cry out in prayer and are persistent in what you ask for, there are no limits to the power of the prayer. Dorothy Norwood sang a song called "I prayed about it." In this song, she stated, "I prayed about it, and he stepped in right on time." I'm a firm believer in the power of prayer, and no one can tell me otherwise.

Chapter 5

I been to jail, and I ain't going back

It was October 28th, 2015, and it was my
20th birthday. This should have been one for
the books, right? Well, it sure was one that I
would never forget. I was feeling better than
ever and had finally reached the dub club. I
was no longer a teenager anymore, and I was
happy about it. The fraternity that I would
later join was having a Halloween party.
Playing football, I had curfew, but this was
one of those nights where I had to set my
own rules. I had done it many times before
and didn't think this night would be any
different. I would sneak out and come back
just in time for workouts the next morning.
As soon as I had made it back to school, I
was shocked to look up and see red and blue

lights in the rear-view mirror. I was very upset but didn't think much of it.

An African American officer approached me and asked for license and registration. I quickly gave them to him. He had a full arm sleeve of tattoos, so I figured he would be cool. Little did I know this man would be the complete opposite. He came back to the car after a few minutes and asked me if I was aware that I had an outstanding warrant. Lying, I said no, and I would take care of it as soon as possible. He had other plans. He said that if it came back from the station that it was legit, then I would be spending the night in jail. I tried to talk my way out of it like I did everything else. I even informed him that I was a football player and had a game in two days, but he did not care. He actually laughed and found entertainment in the situation. To my surprise, I was cuffed very aggressively and thrown in the back of a police cruiser going 100mph in the rural area of Hempstead, TX.

   Hempstead, TX, is in Waller county that is adjacent to Harris County in Houston, TX, and known for the tragic incident involving Sandra Bland. Sandra Bland was a 28-year-old African-American woman who was found hanging in a jail cell in the Waller County jail on July 13, 2015, three days after being arrested during a traffic stop in almost the same spot as me. Her death was ruled a suicide. It was followed by protests against her arrest, disputing the cause of death, and alleging racial violence against her. Bland was pulled over for a traffic violation on July 10. The exchange escalated, resulting in Bland's arrest and she was charged with assaulting a police officer. The arrest was partially recorded by a bystander's cell phone. After authorities reviewed the dashcam footage, the officer was placed on administrative leave for failing to follow proper traffic stop procedures. He was never jailed for any charges. I was in this same spot just a few months later.

This brought fear to my heart. I was afraid to say the least with about how aggressive the officer was with me. Waller County is a rural town, and at 4:00 am, it's a pretty dark and scary place. I didn't know where the officer was speeding to. He pulled up to an old police station that reminded me of a scene from Jeepers Creepers, and I started to get nervous. He said he had to go grab something before he got off. Luckily, he was telling the truth and took me to the Waller

County jail soon after. As soon as I got to the holding cell, I read on the cold wall, "Sandra Bland was here." This sent chills down my body. I was looking to get out of this place as soon as I could. They asked me a series of mental health questions to know if I was thinking about suicide because of the Bland incident. My bond was set at $1,000, and I was ready to make my phone call. I called my mom first, and the system said she did not accept my call. I then called my dad, and the same thing happened. This made me feel as if no one cared for me. I learned later that this was a tactic that they used. My mother informed me that they would not let her accept the call. So, after a few hours, I was sent to the bunk with the other inmates. To my surprise, there were not many inmates there on petty charges. There was some very high risk,

* * *

off the wall criminals, but they were okay people. I met a fellow who was a former KKK member.

While working out with me, he informed me that he was accused of killing a man, but he didn't do it. There were also a couple waiting to go to trial, and also some men who were already sentenced and waiting to be transferred to prison. I even met a young boy who was 17, and I kept in touch with him after I was released. The first day was okay. We played cards and dominos, and everyone told stories about their life on the outside. But by the second day, it had already gotten old for me. The fights over food and not being able to see the daylight began to drive me crazy slowly. Every time I called my parents, I got the same response that they didn't accept the call. I wondered

why no one was answering, so I asked a
sergeant on the floor. He told me that no one
cared about me and that I was just a number
now. He didn't know who I was neither did
he care. He said only the number mattered
and even my name was irrelevant at this
time. This stuck in my head, and after the
third day, I began to believe it. I had not
talked to any member of my family.
Thinking I would be out in a couple of
hours, I was going on my third day there.
I'm not going to say that I was suicidal, but
I would be lying if I said the thought didn't
cross my mind. I finally figured out what
was going on; they forwarded the calls on
purpose. They were holding me, trying to
transfer me to another jail, and that's the
reason my bail was never accepted. I made a
vow that when I got out, I would never do
anything to put myself in that situation

* * *

again. I did a full self-evaluation and asked myself where I wanted to go with my life. Although I was in college, that meant nothing if I was not living up to my full potential. I was finally bailed out Sunday night after getting booked early Thursday morning.

Those four days taught me ultimately where I did not want to end up. I took my freedom for granted and even my life to a certain extent. After talking with those guys in there and them knowing their life on the outside was most likely over, it was like a lightbulb went off in my head. God could have let my bail post as soon as I went in, but I don't think I would have learned my lesson. Staying those four days was enough for him to show me something I wouldn't have been able to see on my own.

* * *

Chapter 6

[L]esson

L is a letter typically used as slang for a loss, whether it be a loss in money or just a setback in life. But as I have grown and shifted into a different mindset, I've concluded that all the losses I have taken have been critical learning lessons. Time after time, I have taken L's. I can remember in high school, our house was burglarized, and I lost the majority of my possessions. One would look at this as a major loss, but this circumstance showed me how real life had become. It showed me the principle of karma, and that whatever goes around comes back around. Some things happen to show you lessons you would have never learned about the karma of the universe. There was a situation when I was in college. I had saved up all my money for a cash car. About $2,400 to be exact, and I was very excited about buying my first car. Unfortunately, I was scammed out of every dime, and to be honest, I wanted to kill the guy at the dealership. The lesson I learned through this situation is that life goes on despite the circumstances. I felt as if some people were supposed to care because I did. I felt as if extreme actions should have been taken.

Honestly, when I ponder back on the situation, I see where I could have been more responsible at the moment. This was when I realized that irresponsibility on your part does not call for an emergency on someone else's behalf. I also learned that I can't act off emotion. I was scammed,

I couldn't go and commit a crime against the person who scammed me. These are two lessons that have stuck with me in my early adult life. This taught me to be more proactive, and most importantly that I can't react any kind of way despite what a person has done to me. Looking at the lesson in every loss teaches you to adapt and stay above the water. We shouldn't ever feel sorry for ourselves because it does nothing for the situation. It's harsh, but tough skin and looking at losses this way can translate into more wins. A loss is merely a mindset that can be changed with proper training.

Chapter 7

The hustler, The scholar

I hold a Bachelor's of Science degree in Computer Engineering from Prairie View A&M University and a Masters of Engineering Management degree from Arkansas State. I have been arrested, detained, and put in jail. I have some friends who are very successful millionaires. I have some family and friends who are convicts and convicted felons. The crazy thing is I love them all the same, and they shaped me to be the man that I am today.

Growing up, I took traits from everyone around me. I was fortunate enough to see who I wanted to be like and who I did not want to be like. I received two educations growing up. One from the streets and the other from the school. That way, I figured I could be twice as smart as everyone else. Meek Mill has a song that debuted in 2014 called "Heaven or Hell" with the lyrics stating, "Some people go to college, some people go to jail, some make it into heaven, and some make it into hell." It might have gone over the head of many, but these lyrics really stuck out to me. Why? Because I feel like he was talking about two different kinds of individuals. Either you are the type to go to college, or maybe you are the type to go to jail. But what if you had been to college and jail. I began to think deeply on the subject. I come from a place where it is lame to go to school but cool to go to jail.

A girl would rather wait on her boyfriend and be loyal to him for going to do a four-year bid in the penitentiary than a full ride football scholarship for four years in my city. I had gone to college, and I had been to jail. I'm very observant and study people a lot. Sometimes I talk a lot, and sometimes I just sit back, observe, and listen. I studied the people in college, and I studied the people in jail. Truth is there was no difference.

One mistake could land you in jail, and that was the bottom line. People in college were committing the same crimes as the people in jail, but they just weren't getting caught. I always say it's not about what you do but how you do it, and that's another major key in this game called life. Frequently I talk to my uncle who is serving a life sentence in prison. He has a major impact on my life. His intellect and knowledge is one like I have never seen before. One greater than any scholar I have

* * *

met at my university or any other. One mistake he made in his early 20s was able to dictate him spending the rest of his life locked up like a zoo animal. I began selling drugs during my 9th- grade year in high school. Many of the people I used to run with back then are now in prison or doing nothing positive with their lives. My mother used to think that my friends were bad influences, but what she didn't know was that I was coming up with all the bad ideas. The difference with me was that even though I was not always doing the right thing, I always was the leader and never the follower. It was through the grace of God that I was never arrested for anything serious.

After all the bad I did, I was arrested for something so petty. I began to think about certain things while sitting in that cell for the

* * *

four days I was incarcerated. It was only God. He was ultimately showing me that if I didn't change my life, this was the place I could be spending a lot more than four days. I listened to the sign, but after a short time, I went back to what I was comfortable with. I'm not the smartest by a long shot, but my ways of working smarter not harder enable me to have the edge over many people.

This has left me with some survivor's guilt. Survivor's guilt, also known as survivor's syndrome, is a mental condition where people believe they did something wrong by surviving an unfortunate event when others did not. This is a very bad case of feeling guilty for others' mistakes. I have always influenced my peers. Some things my old friends are locked up for are things that I introduced them too. I have struggled with this for quite some time, and it seems to get

* * *

worse as I progress in life. Just simple things like scrolling down my Facebook feed to old middle and high school friends seem to get me in my feelings. I tend to wonder what if I didn't show him about drugs or how to commit that crime.

However, even when doing those horrible things, I would always have my grades together. I can think back to the third grade when a couple of classmates and I would get in trouble for talking too much. The teacher would always say that we could talk but only when we finished our book work. What's funny is that I would finish my work first and then distract the other kids from completing their work. This showed early signs that I was a scholar, but that was not who I wanted to be. I always wanted to dumb myself down to make others feel comfortable. It was cool to be ignorant and fit in. Growing up, I just wanted to be cool. Some honest advice for the younger generation is, embrace your differences and don't try to fit in with the crowd. I went to school in the hood for my elementary years.

One thing I can say is that my mom never wanted me to be a product of my environment. So instead of letting me go to my home school, I was enrolled in a better school outside my district. She knew that if I went to school with all my friends, I wouldn't be the best I could be. That was a bright idea because I had already started getting suspended in my later years of elementary school. She sent me to Seminole middle, which was a mixed environment where I knew only a few people. But just like always, I seem to find the wrong crowd time and time again. She had me enrolled in honors classes because my FCAT

(Florida Comprehensive Assessment Test) scores were outstanding the year before. But now, all my new friends were in remedial classes, and I didn't hang out with any of the honors kids. So, I thought I had a brilliant plan. I knew how they would pick students for the honors class the next year.

Knowing that, I purposely changed some answers while taking the exam to get a lower score. Not to my surprise, my plan worked, and when I got my schedule for the next year, I was in remedial classes. I was so happy that I would be in the same classes with all of my friends. This is yet another instance of me doing things to fit in with the wrong crowd instead of being myself. That year, I got in the most trouble ever. I got suspended multiple times and began smoking marijuana at the age of thirteen.

* * *

Despite all the trouble, I still managed to keep a 3.0 GPA, and please don't ask me how because I honestly don't know. Everyone I was hanging out with had low grades, and some were even kicked out because of this. God kept me afloat even when I was trying to sink my own ship. We used my grandma's address for me to attend that school, so unlike the other kids, I didn't have a school bus to take. I took the city bus to and from school every day. One day I had misplaced my bus card and needed to get to school. At this time, stealing bikes was the thing to do, and I had done this many times before. But for some reason, there were no bicycles in any of the yards on the way to my school this day. I finally found a bike, but it was behind a fence. After looking for more, I saw that it was the only bike on the street so I had to do what

I had to do.

After jumping the fence, I failed to realize the bike's tire was flat. Then a voice yelled, "Get out of my yard." I jumped the fence and took off running. I still have the cut on my hand till this date from jumping the fence, even though this was about 8-9 years ago. I ran for about half a mile and thought the coast was clear after I switched streets. Then looking down I glanced up, I saw a Jamaican man with long dreadlocks and light brown eyes pointing a shotgun at me through the window of his car. He asked how would my mother like it if he took my life. I told him she wouldn't like it at all. He asked me why I was trying to steal his bike, and I replied that I was just trying to get to school. He told me that if I continued down the path I was on, I would be dead or in jail.

This was a near death experience with God sparing my life, but I took this too for granted. I was still in love with money and had no real positive influences. I then found myself doing whatever I had to do to get some money and realizing that I didn't even have a conscience.

Despite all the negativity, God was still blessing me. I was playing JV football but never had any playing time, so I was thinking of quitting that too. The JV season ended, and the coach asked who would like to go up to varsity to essentially be practice dummies. Being fearless as I always was, I did it. Not to my surprise but to everyone else's, I ran all over our varsity's defense in practice. I found myself now in a situation that I had never been in before. This was when I began to love football. I had always played football, but it was always just a hobby. After my little success, I then became obsessed with improvement. Over the summer, I put in numerous hours watching YouTube videos and improving my game. With me putting all this time into football, I had little time to do any wrong. I then began to change my friends from thugs to other football players, and this was essential to me becoming who I am today. The company you keep plays a big role in where your interest lies.

If you hang around the barbershop long enough, you will eventually want a haircut. I was not the biggest, strongest, or most talented, but I began to become a master of my craft. Not only on the field but also in the classroom. Like I said, I have always been smart but never really put effort into it.

* * *

But as I began to do right, God always had a way of shining his light on me. In the 11th grade, I found myself as the starting running back on the varsity football team with a 3.7 GPA. I was now gaining interest from top tier academic institutions. This always went over my head though. I didn't want to go to an Ivy League school because it was never my goal to be a scholar, and I never really thought about it too much.

Somehow, my plans always take a backseat to God's plans. Although I didn't attend an Ivy League school, the Roy G Perry College of Engineering is one of the top engincering programs in the country. I was challenged in ways I had never been before, and again to my surprise, I found myself doing it by accident. Playing football and focusing on doing the right thing,

I was awarded the highest GPA award for computer engineering for the class of 2017. I won the Athletic Black Engineer of the Year award at the BEYA (Becoming Everything You Are) conference. I had NFL dreams, and although my grades were great, I never cared about school. Thinking back on it, God had been showing me I had a gift and how to use it. I never wanted to work hard and apply myself in the classroom like I was on the football field. I even had a successful sneaker selling business in college. The hustle has always been real. However, in college, I found myself barely getting by after my recent success and now reverting to some bad habits and finding myself in sticky situations. I once was the starting running back with a very promising future. Even while doing everything right and giving it my all, God had other plans. In the matter of one year, I had gone from being the starting running back to barely playing. A series of unfortunate events occurred, and I ended up losing my scholarship and having to revert to my academics to pay for my school. Thankfully, I was still doing just enough to get by. Now with a baby on the way, I was forced to quit the football team and work two jobs to make ends meet. It wasn't until this time I was then forced to take my education seriously. I was forced to be great in academics for the first time in my life. I learned that to graduate on time, I had to take a full course load and five hours online. I was now a full-time student and a full-time employee. This was the first semester I ever took serious focusing on school. I received a 3.9 GPA that semester, and this was when I declared to myself that I was a scholar. This GPA was even higher than it was when I received the award. After graduating, I decided to pursue grad school while being a full-time engineer. Throughout grad school, I answered the calling that God was always trying to show me, and I received straight A's the first time in my life. I declared myself as the Hood Scholar and found that when I put my mind to something, I can accomplish anything with God.

Chapter 8

How it all began

Growing up, I remember people always asking me what I wanted to be when I grew up. Honestly, I didn't have a clue. The normal person would look to their role models to shape them into the man that they wanted to be, right? Imagine having no role model, no one who had any real influence. I had heard stories of how my dad had money years ago, but once he got out of prison and decided to change his life for the better, that was no more than a distant memory. With everyone struggling and living paycheck to paycheck, my role models became the people who had money, who were the hustlers.

This is the time in my life when I became infatuated with the streets.

Whoever had the nicest cars, clothes, and women is who I strived to be like. A product of my environment is what I would become. I had never been a bad kid, but when you are from where I'm from, the environment can tend to get the best of you. Some might not understand, but if you have parents with good jobs or both parents in the home, you can easily look at crime and wonder why people are doing these crazy things. As I have progressed further in life, I too am guilty of forgetting those days when the lights or water were turned off. How easily do we tend to forget? It's very easy to look at people struggling and say there must be a reason why they are in that position. It is also easy to look from their point of view and ask why was I was dealt the short end of the stick in life? I pondered on this subject and concluded that there is no such thing as the short end of the stick. Every man has the same 24 hours, and what you spend your time on most likely will dictate your destiny. Earlier this week, I came across a post on social media saying how can we have billionaires in a world where kids are starving. This bothers me. Instead of trying to make a change in our situation, we as people would rather sit and count the next man's pockets.

You should never let your plate get cold while watching someone else eat. We know not of the trials and tribulations the billionaires had to go through or what adversities they faced. A study of millionaires was conducted, and it

* * *

was found that more than 70% of millionaires in 2017 were first generation.

This alone should ensure us that if we focus on our craft and not worry about what everyone else is doing, we could attain generational wealth as well. I value my life the same as the rich man. He is no better than me and puts his pants on one leg at a time just like me. Once everyone realizes this theory, I believe they will have no choice but to be better off. We can't feel sorry for ourselves, because I'm not sure if anyone told you, but the sad thing is no one even cares. We as people are more versatile than any other race. I have a family member who has been in and out of jail for the past five years. The crazy thing is I'm an engineer, and he quite frankly might be smarter than me. Filled with talent, he is book smart and has natural talents. He can cut hair, draw tattoos, and was one heck of a quarterback in high school. He went wrong by trying to rush life. Instead of waiting it out and going through the process, he decided to speed up his life. When we rush life, we usually end up in places we have no business being in. Now he's in and out of jail and spends his time reminiscing about what he could have done. I even sometimes catch him speaking on how others don't deserve their success and blaming other people for his decisions. We must wake up and take responsibilities for our actions. We must take responsibility and hold ourselves to higher standards and have faith that we can make a change.

Chapter 9

Doctors hang with doctors

This is a term me and my friends began using in high school. Early on, it was just fun and games. We used to refer to this term to talk about girls. Basically, what the term meant was that if a girl's friend is promiscuous, then she would be too. This has stuck with us throughout the years. The meaning has changed, but the concept remains the same. A wise man once told me, t if there are five broke people you are hanging around, then you will eventually become the sixth. If you spend your time around five millionaires, you will have a good chance of becoming the sixth. You are the company you keep. You are your friends.

To elevate in life, you should have good company. I have been struggling with this for quite some time now. In every stage in life, I tend to grow, and while growing, I always seem to outgrow my friends. Not that they are not my friends and I don't love them, but it's just that I'm obsessed with improvement.

I have been living through the phrase "if you are not getting better, you are getting worse" for about ten years now. My biggest fear in life is being average. When I feel myself getting complacent, I must make a move to assure that this never happens. It may sound bad, but you are the director of your own life, if something or someone has to get cut, it's strictly business. On this journey, I have lost lots of friends and even some family members. Sometimes I feel bad, but at the end of the day, it's strictly business. I know for me that to be my best self, I have to live life a certain way. I found myself always caring for the well- being of others before myself, and that was my biggest mistake. Wanting more success for a person than they want for themselves is an up and coming train wreck.

My new circle of friends, although very tight, is filled with people who have a lot of the same values as me. Everyone is hardworking and very passionate about what they do. You should never feel like you can't learn from your friends. At that point it is time to change your surroundings. If your friends don't motivate you, that's a sign you should have different friends. I recently did a study on the law of attraction. The law of attraction is defined as the ability to attract into your life whatever you are focusing on. I believe this is an underrated cheat code to life. No matter the religion or ethnicity, the law of attraction is very important but also one of life's biggest mysteries. The most challenging part of acknowledging and accepting the truth of what the law of attraction has to offer is realizing that every single one of your decisions in life, good or bad, have been shaped by you alone. Quite scary but also interesting. Life is crazy, and you must be careful about every decision. You must think first before you make any action or even more important any reaction. Your thoughts and company will eventually turn into reality. Focusing on the negative things will keep you down and under a cloud of negative energy. Proverbs 23:7 says, "For as a man thinketh in his heart, so is he." Your thoughts come to real life.

There is power in the tongue, and I tell people this all the time, don't be surprised when the things you say with your mouth, whether negative or positive, come true. I try only to speak positively about everyone and every situation. Winners win, and losers lose. I feel that for you to be your best self, you must surround yourself with winners in your circle and positive thoughts in your mind.

Part 2: Principles
Chapter 10

Faith it til' you make it

Knowing God from a good place thrives us to want to know God better. When wanting to know God on a higher level, He tends to show us how mighty he really is. I call it the faith test, which is much harder than any standardized test we have ever taken. We must be confident in the crisis. Faith and plenty of prayers gave me a sense of certainty that I wasn't alone. Faith helped me connect to the power source to get over, through, and around the hard times. We must encourage ourselves. Look yourself in the mirror and tell yourself you know you can accomplish any task at hand. Don't get caught up in worrying where you are at now that you can't see that God is with you.

* * *

Weeping may endure for a night but joy cometh in the morning. It may be painful, but it's necessary. My old high school coach had a saying that I refer to almost weekly. He used to tell us, "Life is hard, but it is also fair." I took heed and continued to believe, no matter how hard the task or how far away the outcome may seem. To essentially grow our faith, we must first believe it ourselves.

If you can believe it, you can achieve it. Despite other people's thinking, if you have a vision, you must believe in yourself. I can think back to when I was playing football and had no choice but to faith it until I made it. I was 5'6'' 165 lbs. and maybe 5'7'' on a good day. To the naked eye and a lot of the people around me, I would never get a scholarship to play division one football.

But the first person and the only person who needed to believe in Jovante Ham was Jovante Ham. I believed, and I worked. I believed, then I worked some more. That strong faith led me to involve myself in an environment where I could make my dream come true. Low faith or believing what other people told me could have led me to throw in the towel years before I received the blessing. The enemy plays mind tricks. It is up to us to realize him and counter the attacks with our positive faith. A recent study conducted on successful entrepreneurs said that 97% of the people who gave up are employed by the 3% that didn't. This is something I think about almost every day in the early stages of my business. Sometimes it might be a situation or task we set out to accomplish, and we knew we could do it.

As we approach the goal, there is sometimes a sense of cold feet that we might get. That is fine, but when our cold feet become doubt is where the problem lies. We must rely on the faith that rose in us to start the task. Faith it til' you make it is not as easy as it sounds. A hundred percent of people who have the strongest faith have gone through situations that brought them to this place. I see faith as another muscle in the body.

Just like any other muscle, it should be worked out regularly to become strong. God will take you on a detoured route a lot of the times to test you while building your faith at the same time. My faith had grown the most in times when I had no other choice but to believe even what I couldn't see. The times when one's next move is out of his or her control is one of the hardest situations I have ever faced to date. One thing about it, whatever happens eventually happens. It may not be on our time, but it always happens on time. Once we make it to our destination and look back and see all the adversity we overcame, we are far more appreciative. I take pride in taking the long route with no shortcuts. Your faith may waiver and get light at times, but if you don't give up, you can accomplish anything. I encourage you to keep a faith file in the back of your mind, remembering all the times God took care of you. I am nowhere near where I want to be in my faith, but I am striving to get there every day. A vision of faith in a perfect world for me would be blindfolding yourself and walking across the busiest highway and knowing that God can and will deliver you to the other side of the road.

Chapter 11

Money ain't everything

CREAM. Cash Rules Everything Around Me. I used to be addicted to money and would do anything for money, even steal for money.

Why? It is merely a piece of paper with a slave master on it, but this same piece of paper has sent many of God's children home quite early. I had a friend who was a very great athlete. Through a series of unfortunate events, he was unable to accept his scholarship offer. Football was all he knew, and it was promising that he would make it to the NFL. Once reality set in and those dreams were gone, he reverted to the only way he knew to get money, robbing people. Sad to say, he eventually tried to rob the

* * *

wrong person and was shot and killed. He left behind a beautiful daughter. I ask the question for what. This same piece of green paper. I sometimes wonder why he chose that route. What would he have bought with the money if the operation had been successful? Was it worth it? This piece of paper was the reason this young girl no longer had her father.

In the Bible, 1 Timothy 6:10 says: "The love of money is the root of all evil." How can we love such a thing? Love is defined as an intense feeling of deep affection. How can we love something that can't love us back? Is money really that important? While broke, I would always wonder, "Man, how would it feel to have a lot of money?" Now that I have money, I've realized you still will feel the same way. If you were a sad person before, you would remain a sad person after you have money and vice versa. It's merely a piece of paper. I try to explain this concept to people, and they tell me it's only because I have money. While they might be right, the main point is that it's not worth all the trouble we go through to obtain it.

Many have ended up in jail or even worse, a grave, all for a piece of paper that's going to be recycled anyway. Although it may be hard to believe, but you heard it from here first. Money is indeed something, but it's not everything. We should strive to live a blessed life, and a blessed life is far more than a fat wallet.

Chapter 12

Life from Both Sides

I have been blessed to have the opportunity to see life from both sides of the fence. Other than love while growing up, my family had nothing. No one owned a house, car, or anything for that matter. Food stamps, section 8, and housing projects were normal, and I never saw a problem with these forms of government assistance. South Florida is big but other than the tri- county area, a lot of us have never been outside of Palm Beach County. Despite a few family reunions in Georgia and South Carolina, I too had never been past Palm Beach. Even when we visited family members in other states, the living situations were very similar.

Sometimes when people asked me what I wanted to be when I got older, I told them that I wanted to be a garbage man because of a close friend's father. He was a garbage man, cut hair on the side, and had a wife who was a school secretary. They seemed to have it all together. He would get lots of things for Christmas. Now that I look back on it, it was just because it was a two-parent household with multiple incomes. This is very rare where I am from.

Aside from that friend, I don't know anyone who was married or whose parents were even still together. This was normal, and if you didn't know any better, you would think that it's the way life is supposed to go. These underlying factors make the struggle real. If your mother is working two jobs, and your father is dead or in jail, the question becomes "who will

● ● ●

babysit?". This is a repeat cycle in urban neighborhoods around the country, and these are all reasons for the living conditions of my environment. It's normal for teens to get pregnant. It's normal for them to be single. It's normal to be a grandma at 32. The thing is that we don't complain about it because that is just the hand we were dealt. I know people struggling at the bottom, who have more fun every day than many successful people who you would believe have it all.

This was so intriguing to me, and I wanted to get down to the source of this issue. Everyone's goal is to make it out of the hood and be rich, right? Growing up, I would always hear the phrase, "When I get rich." People would say when I get rich, everything will be okay, and my whole family will be good.

They would say when I get rich, I am going
to buy this, or when I get rich, I'm going to
buy that. People have this impression that
money will solve all their problems. I hate to
be the bearer of bad news, but this is nothing
but a fairy tale. I am speaking from personal
experience of situations that I have seen
firsthand with either family or friends.
Christmas is my favorite time of the year,
and the season itself just gives off the spirit
of love. In my environment, Christmas
could either be a good time or a bad time,
depending on the circumstances of your
family. In the hood, there aren't any big
Christmas trees or grandparents coming to
visit for the holidays and bringing presents
for everyone. There was no eggnog,
Christmas carols, or presents under the tree.
I remember the times my mom scraped

up all her money just to get presents under the tree the day before Christmas. Sometimes on a bad Christmas, a common phrase would be, "When I get my income tax." In my community, income tax season is more of a celebration and holiday than Christmas. According to Investopedia.com, a tax refund is defined as a refund on taxes paid to an individual or household when the actual tax liability is less than the total amount of taxes paid during the tax year. A tax refund results from a refundable tax credit that reduces a taxpayer's bill below zero. The more children you have, the more money you get back on your tax refund. I have heard people jokingly say that they were only having children to get more money when tax season arrives again. A good friend of mine always told me to pay close attention because there is a little truth in every joke.

Having a child for an extra $2,000 sounds crazy, but I can assure these are situations going on this very moment. We find ourselves looking forward to the big payday and sometimes even spending the money before we receive it. In my neighborhood, they even have check cashing stores that when you show them how much you will receive and give you the amount. So rather than waiting an extra three weeks, we are willing to pay a ridiculous interest rate. I can recall a situation last year when a young woman who was a single mother bragged to her then coworker and friend about how she would be receiving $7,000 on her tax refund. Her friend then setup a "master plan." She told her boyfriend and another individual about her friend receiving the large lump sum of cash, and they planned to rob the woman. The plan went a little past their expectation, and during the struggle, the woman was shot and killed by the gunman. Now I'm no rocket scientist, but $7,000 divided by three is less than $2,500. Three children are without a mother and a father for a lousy $2,333, and that's if they were going to split the money three ways. For you to take someone's life for that amount of money bothers me and gives me a funny feeling on the inside.

Before I went to college and saw the bigger picture, I too thought that it was a lot of money. However, the point is that a life was taken for that amount or even any amount of money. I always wondered if I could talk with the three co-defendants to see their reasoning and ask them so now you have the money, now what? I wonder, would they take their own kids on a shopping spree or buy a lot of marijuana or maybe even buy rims for their car? This leads right into my next point, which is that I don't believe the problem in my community is the money but the mindset. Lots of people cry and complain about money. I'm always hearing, "If I had money, I would buy this, or if I had money, I would buy that." I have seen situations where whether it be the lotto, insurance settlements, or any large lump sum of money. I have a family member who makes probably no more than $20,000 annually. There was a car wreck, and they settled to get $10,000. Within a span of months, she was broke. How? She bought a new car, every new pair of shoes, and began lending money out to various family members. I began to think if money was really the problem. I took a survey asking

* * *

people what they would do if they had won $20,000. Almost everyone said that they would either buy a new car or go shopping. Not one person said they would buy some land or invest their money in the stock market. The problem is deeper than the source. We never learn about investing in the stock market or real estate. Everyone wants to be hood rich. The difference with me is that I didn't want to be hood rich. I wanted to be rich for real. Hood rich is $10,000 cash flexing in pictures for the internet. Most of my family and old friends who hustle around the way don't even own a vehicle, and some are still living with their parents. What we must do is outthink our environment to be great. Playing college football, we would always talk of this. I played division one football at Prairie View A&M, which is an HBCU a little outside of Houston.

* * *

We competed in the South Western Athletic conference, better known as the SWAC. When training, we always wanted to be great. We all believed that we could and should have been playing FBS, which is big time division one football. One way to prove this was that we would train like we were at an Alabama or LSU because we understood that even if we were doing well in the SWAC, our goal was to make it to the NFL. At that stage, no one cared where you went to college because everyone is equal. This theory lines up right along with real life with me coming out of that environment. I knew that if I wanted to be successful, I wasn't competing with the people in my neighborhood but people across the country. Everyone from the neighborhood knows me as one of the most hardworking people they know. They always ask me why I'm never resting and why I'm always working hard. I simply believe that I'm not trying to outwork the people in my environment but the environment that I look forward to being in.

Chapter 13

The other side

Until I got a job in Corporate America, I
had never really known a white person.
Sure, I had had teachers and people I ran
into daily, but as a true friend, I never had
one. It's quite hard to understand someone
who you never sat down and had a real
conversation with. The question that was
burning my insides was, "Where did we go
wrong as a race?" I wouldn't say that the
entire Caucasian population is successful,
but there was indeed something that they
were doing that we were not. A couple of
months into on the job, I became friends
with the first person I could call "a friend of
the other race." We began to discuss issues,
and how his family became successful.

* * *

He told me of how his family owned a business. He also told me how his parents were happy at home, and his life was filled with love. He had never known anyone who had been shot or killed. He had faced no trauma in life, and up until his grandmother died when he was 24, he had never experienced death. He knew no one in prison or who had ever committed a crime. He explained how his parents had met in college and were very well off. I told him how I had experienced death from a first-person view and couldn't count on two hands how many people I knew that were murdered. He couldn't believe me. This is something that we made normal in our community, and we are the ones to blame. More role models that motivate the children to do the right thing is what we need. Everyone taking the easy route that will do nothing but create a repeat cycle. If a child sees his father or mother doing something, nine times out of ten, when they are old enough, they will follow suit. I thank God my father left the streets alone for his children's sake because I too could have been further off the path than I already was. He explained how his family viewed us as a race, and quite frankly, I had to agree. He spoke on how they felt we were lazy and would rather depend on the government than to get a job. Nothing comes overnight, and we must realize that. We make excuses for why this person became successful. We say how most of these people were born into success or money. I take the Kylie Jenner controversy, for example. Kylie recently became the youngest self-made billionaire.

Instead of congratulating her for this achievement, our race would rather spread hate, trying to dim her light by saying she was born into money. What most people don't realize is how much a billion dollars is, one thousand million, and if Kim Kardashian net worth is not even $400 million, that should tell you that it had almost nothing to do with the inheritance.

Her older sister, Kendall, has a net worth of $22 million, and they received the same inheritance. Granted, that's a lot of money, but we must stop doing this. I look at it like this: If she did it, I can do it too.

Most people can never get things into this mindset. They would rather hate and make excuses and I believe this is one of our main problems. With that negative mindset, we will never achieve greatness. I'm never in denial about things, and I am honest with myself first. The things we do start from top to down, and we must change ourselves first. Before we complain about the circumstances, we must look at how we got there and what we can do in our immediate lives to fix it. My coworker's family didn't always have money, but it started with one generation that wanted to make a change, and that's what they did. Although our circumstances might be quite a bit worse, the past can't be fixed, but we must start with wanting more for ourselves. As a race, we have to value things finished over things started. We can do anything we put our minds to, and we must remember we can do all things through Christ who strengthens us.

Chapter 14

Generational Curse

History is repeating itself at an all-time high. Granted, things are happening in this day and age that would have never happened in previous generations, but the narrative remains the same. We are moving in circles when it comes to a race. Sure, a few people are making it out of their situations, but the next generation is in jeopardy of not withholding it. We are living in the time where it is easier than ever to be an overnight star. But instead of taking advantage of their current situation, we rather waste the money on material things that won't be relevant five years from now. Too many liabilities and not enough assets is our problem. I have a family friend who made it to the NFL. Fast forward twenty years later, he is broke and back to square one.

As soon as we get an expandable amount of money, we spend it on the silliest of things. I challenge our generation to change the culture. Own something, unlike our parents and grandparents and leave something behind for your kids. Everyone complains about their situation but takes no affirmative action to fix the problem. We must stop spending money on things to impress people who could care less about us. I would think that this was just something young people did, but it's sad to say we are just picking up where our parents left off. We can't expect to receive different results from making the same mistakes they did. We can observe how other races come right

* * *

into our neighborhoods and build million-dollar businesses. Why can't we do the same?

Besides, most of the time, they are foreigners who came to the states with nothing. So, what's our excuse? Slavery? That was over 400 years ago. It might sound harsh, but we must do better. I would like to see our generation investing in ourselves more and going against the grain. It's okay to be different and do something no one has ever done. There has to come a point when we get tired of living in poverty. We might think that we are getting over on the government by receiving assistance when they are bird feeding us, to be completely honest. There is so much more to the world than the neighborhood your family is renting in. I encourage you to travel and see all life has to offer. This is a big world, and I believe we should have the same opportunities as everyone else and explore it. We have to make up our mind that we want it first and then we must act. For instance, it's okay to get married. We are living in a world where marriage rates are at an all-time low. When two people join in love for the same cause they are a force to be reckoned with. It's very hard to do it by yourself despite your salary. I began to think differently and was encouraged to do the things no one else was doing. I want to be different than everyone who got it wrong in my family. To do this, we must stand up and go against the odds to break all the generational curses.

Chapter 15

I made it out

"I made it out the hood, Forget a Grammy."

-Young Jeezy

Making it out of a place where very few have the privilege to has its pros and cons. Remember the times of dreaming and praying to make it out of the hood, and now you have found yourself right amid your dreams. We all have imagined making it and being the answer to everyone's problems. Needless to say, the process didn't quite work out as planned. Throughout the journey, many left you when you were down. People began to talk, and sometimes you may feel bad that you made it and someone else didn't. We all have the same

24 hours, and it's up to us how we attack each day. Jay Z once said, "People look at you strange, saying you changed like you worked that hard to stay the same." I really love this quote because it's one of the realest things ever said. We work hard for results, and with results come change.

It is said that a man at 40 years old thinking like he did at 20 years old had essentially wasted 20 years of his life. One of the biggest problems I have seen by making it out of the hood is the envy and hate by your peers. By peers, I mean former friends and associates you grew up with. If anything, you would think these would be the main people rooting for you. Sadly, this is true too many times. They might say you're acting funny just by trying to better yourself. I wanted to dig into what the problem was. It really bothered me that the people that are supposed to be the proudest of you talk about you the most.

After studying successful people and those who had potential but felt as if they never lived up to it, I concluded the thought, People may envy your life because they see through you what they could have been. Many of the times similar to my situation and many others, the people hating often had better opportunities than me. I can recall someone with whom I used to be friends with in grade school. He was a better football player than me back then. Very talented fellow, but as we got into high school, I began to be the better player. There was only one reason for this, and that was hard work beats talent when talent doesn't work hard. Making the long story short, he began to hate and live off the fame he had from little league. I was awarded a scholarship, and he wasn't. Although being best friends, I heard friends from back home saying that he was really hating on me. They told me some of his comments.

For instance, I was told he said that if he would've worked hard, I would have never gone to college because he would've had the show. He also spoke that I would never make it to the NFL because I was not better than him. But in my face, none of these comments ever surfaced. He was right about the NFL comment though and you may think I'm lying when I tell you that I'm happy for it. Football was all I had. It was my first love and was my top priority in life. I am from a society where people don't think you are doing much in life if you are not an athlete or rapper. They believe those are the only ways to become successful in life. What they fail to realize is that a silent millionaire is lethal. I would rather have success than fame any day. Taking the route I took and having a promising football career crumble before my eyes, one might think I had failed in life.

From this exact situation, I was forced to explore more of my talents than running and jumping. I was challenged to use my mind. This situation broadened my horizon and gave me the perspective that If I worked hard enough, I could own a team. When I walked away from football during my senior year in college, people couldn't see my vision. In the end tough, the only person that needed to believe in it was me. I was determined to be successful, and I had to cut ties with anything that was holding me back from greatness. I felt as if I had gotten all I could get out of the sport and it was time for the next chapter. I shifted my focus but kept the same mindset and work ethic. Before I knew it, I began to blossom, and those same traits I always showed on the football field began to help me in life. The discipline, hard work, and dedication I learned throughout my 18-year football career were second to none. Lebron James said that we need less LeBron's and more engineers, teachers, and police officers. Any time we are using our bodies for income, there is an expiration date no matter the task. However, when using the brain for income, we will be better off and able to control our destiny. We all grew up with the dream of making it out the hood. We were all given the impression that the only ways to make it out were by either rapping, playing ball, or selling dope.

The crazy thing is that there are a million ways to make money. We have to teach young kids the way to go. If you can sell drugs, you can start a business. If you can write a rap, you can write a book. If you can survive in the projects, you can survive in Corporate America. I wouldn't tell you it can't be done if I didn't do it myself. I was blessed with a gift to make money. A natural born hustler. I had been selling candy since grade school. I have done everything from selling drugs to pimping women. I have done white collar crimes all the way to burglary. I'm not ashamed to tell anyone of my past. The reason for this is because I want to encourage the next generation that they don't have to make this mistake. All we must do is be resilient in all things. The same way we strive to get

* * *

credentials in the streets and hustle must be the same way we strive to be successful in our day to day lives. Wake up with an urge for someone to know your name. We overlook them, but the same principles are used in both areas. The stock market is nothing but a legal dope game buying low to sell high. We must attack everything with the same mindset. All it takes is a slight amount of hope. The hope then becomes faith. I encourage you to dream big because when dreaming big, it deletes all fears of failure. I made it out, and I'm determined to get more people to realize they can too. There are so many ways to make it out. We can't get caught in the crossfire of the world. To look like you are successful and be successful are two different things. Don't let anyone discourage you, and the most important thing is don't ever feel bad when

● ● ●

you do make it because you worked hard for it.

Chapter 16

Crabs in a bucket

We are living in quite a time these days. We hate the celebrities for the life they live and even hate on the people we grew up with our whole life. This crabs in a bucket mentality must stop. I believe one of the reasons I am blessed is because I love to see everyone win. I never hate on the next man but simply wait my turn. I could never understand what is so hard about this concept. Maybe it is our selfish human nature. People act like there isn't enough money or success to go around. But then again, they say that misery loves company. We can take for example, a close friend of mine who had a bright future in the NFL ahead of him. He got into some legal trouble and was kicked out of school. Instead of sending him encouraging words of wisdom, people in our own community laughed at him. The crazy thing is those are some of the same people who we had grown with. It was hard to tell that those were supposed to be the same people that should be proud of him. It's hard enough to make it out and even when someone does it's your own people to tear you down. We then get mad and say this person doesn't give back to the community.

Maybe if we had genuine support, people would come back and do more. I will say this time and time again throughout the text, and I'll say it again here, we must stop comparing and contrasting our lives. It may be something as simple as we see that we could've or should've been in that's person shoes. Thing is we were not, so we have to play the hand that we were dealt. I don't mind working for my blessing. Lots of people talk bad about the people who make it out but wouldn't dare make the sacrifices the person who made it out would. I got into an argument in college with a non-athlete. She told me that football players didn't deserve to get our school payed for and should be in debt like the rest of the students. I then asked her would she be willing to wake up at 4 a.m., head straight to workouts, finish, and go eat breakfast. After breakfast, attend three to four classes consecutively, go to lunch and maybe another class after that, then head straight to practice, after practice head to dinner followed by team meetings.

• • •

We sometimes wouldn't get home until 9 or 10 o'clock. She didn't understand that we did a lot more than run and jump. Then I realized that it could be that people fear and despise what they don't understand. If they knew the sacrifices and the discipline it took to accomplish the lifestyle they hated on, then maybe they would respect it more. Lots of people aren't fond of Floyd Mayweather because he is cocky and arrogant. They say he doesn't deserve all of his money and so on. What they don't see is the countless hours of training that he partakes in. It costs to be the boss. Discipline defines your destiny. So instead of talking down and not being happy for someone who is at a place you desire to be, try to figure out what traits or characteristics they practice on the daily. This will do you far more than wishing on someone's downfall and hating on them.

* * *

We all have the same 24 hours and it's up to you to take advantage of it.

Chapter 17

Different Level Different Devil

For every level, there is always another devil. The anointing on your life attracts attacks, especially when leveling up. I have seen that once you begin to take a leap up, things occur to try to knock you back down. Some say it's like taking a step forward and two steps back. Now I know that the enemy hates success, but even when the enemy is working hard, God is always pulling the other side of the rope a tad bit harder. The enemy knows our weaknesses and how he can get to us. Maybe I should rephrase that and say "how he thinks he can get to us." After leveling up and getting closer to the higher power, certain things won't bother us like how they used to. He knows this, and he makes a way in any situation, whether spouse, family, finances, and much more. He knows every situation and will tend to pick at the thing he knows might send us right back to the old us.

When growing, we should pride our self in recognizing the enemy's attack and not allow him to send us backwards. Life is ultimately a game that we must strategize and think before every move we make. He is playing chess, so we must learn to play chess also. Mindset mentality and staying focused is key. Even when the enemy thinks he is on the operating table, we must know that while we are fighting for our life, God is with us and working in the waiting room. We must work smarter and not harder. We must also remember to do our part and know that we are in a two on one matchup against the enemy. I feel we have to do our part and leave the rest to God. We can only control what we can control. Lots of people use the term "more money more problems." This too is a form of different level different devil. If praying for things like a business or financial increase, one must know that you won't have the same problems you once had. Problems can graduate. Whether physically, mentally, or spiritually, there are different levels to each of these. He attacks most, if not all, these areas at once. I can tell you he hates the glory being given to God more than anything. When we thank God for blessings and speak that we know God was the reason for the level of increase, it irks him. He then now wants to trigger a relapse and send you back to the old place and lower if he can. We can't let him in and recognize this is just a new devil for the new level we have reached.

Chapter 18

Patience is a Virtue

Some say patience is a virtue, and this has been the story of my life time after time. But I'm here to tell you that what is for you is for you. Patience is said not to be the ability to wait but our behavior in the season of waiting. This popcorn society of wanting everything fast has taken the glory out of the process. If everything comes so quick, you will not appreciate it because it was attained so easily. Growing up, I always heard the saying, "good things come to those who wait." It wasn't until I had made mistakes that it really clicked in my head. I remember buying my first car. I was so eager and ready to shine because I had seen everyone else driving their cars. As soon as I had two nickels to rub together, I was at the car lot. Without even checking the carfax, I bought my first car with no hesitation from a previous owner online. It was a 2012 Volkswagen CC Sport. No more than 30 days later, the motor was blown, and I was all out of money. I had no money to repair it. I think back and wish I had never bought the car. I had the cash and could have gotten a reasonable cash car. But instead, I was so infatuated with driving a foreign car that I didn't want to advice that told me otherwise. I wanted to show off and impress the other kids at school, and boy did I learn my lesson about that. Your time is your time. We can't compare our current situation to the next person's. It's kind of like comparing someone else's chapter 20 to our chapter 10. We should never be jealous of the next persons success because I can assure you that as long as you stay down, your time is coming. I never understood the type of people who tried to dim another person's lightbulb to make theirs shine brighter. I was always the type who wants everyone to win, but I also wanted to win and would always find myself saying, "I can't wait for my turn." There was a time in my early adult life when I was watching almost everyone around me become successful. I was at a place where I didn't like who I was. I felt as if everyone was becoming greater while I was kind of at a standstill. I then began to try and rush my process, and that is where I crashed out. Trying to make things better, I did nothing but made the situation much worse. Patience is one of the most important traits, not only for becoming successful but in life itself. It is an absolute requirement to attain your goals because when you do get that thing you set out for today, you have to be patient to get back to it tomorrow. Patience is proactive and takes involvement and much detail. When my daughter's mother was pregnant, we always stressed how we couldn't wait until she had the baby. The truth was the baby wasn't ready for the world. It took my daughter almost ten months to be formed and shaped into the beautiful bundle of joy that we know today. Even if she had come a week earlier, something wouldn't have been incomplete. This is how we must look at the waiting season. During the wait, you are being shaped into a better version of you. I like to call it, "you 2.0." Remember those things you were praying for and got a little angry when they weren't answered. I can testify that I have been in this predicament several times before. When looking back, you say things like, "I know why I received a no." I had brilliant ideas to make money in my college years. Ideas that I believed could've been million-dollar businesses, but I could never seem to keep the money I had saved for the business. I would always cap out and never exceed the amount. I also had a problem with going to the strip club almost every night. If I had become successful at this time, it's no telling where I might be today. God was shaping my discipline and core values into what they are today. I couldn't wait at a stoplight without cursing up a storm. Other people also need our patience. Road rage has caused a lot of people to leave this earth a lot sooner than they probably would have because of impatience by either part.

Going to college might be the biggest test of patience I have ever gone through. Being broke while watching others who I grew up with sell drugs, do credit card scams, and get all the appealing women was very tempting. I even got off track a couple of times for these same issues. I had to find out the hard way that fast money doesn't last long. And to be quite honest, the hard-earned money is even hard to hold on to. It wasn't until a lot of those same friends ended up either dead or in prison that I valued my patience the most. We must realize that patience is nothing more than a state of mind. It is indeed something that builds progress over time, and if we keep working at it, we will nourish it more and more. You must be careful not to use patience as an excuse in certain situations. Don't use patience as an

• • •

excuse for procrastination or perfectionism. We have to be our own judge of patience and measure it on a case by case basis. We should instead use patience for gaining clarity, self-reflection, and making the most out of every opportunity we are faced with.

Chapter 19

Progress over pride

Pride derives from the French word "prud," which is a late Old English word variously translated as "excellent, splendid, arrogant, haughty." It is thought as "having a high opinion of oneself." Pride is an inward emotion of deep pleasure of a corrupted sense of one's personal value. Progress is the movement towards an improved or developed state. I don't know about you, but my pride has hindered my progress too many times. We often let pride hinder our progress in situations by being stubborn. Pride is an action in our minds; however, it can hinder our body and spirit. Our minds and our bodies are so close that they can transmit each other's diseases. Pride can keep you from physical and mental growth. This can indeed kill you.

Pride can keep you from many things. Pride can cause us to filter out God in certain situations. Pride can cause you to neglect others that you know can help you in certain situations. I am guilty of cutting someone all the way off once they have shown me their true colors. I am still working on this issue today because it seems I can act as if a person never existed in my life. This form of pride I believe is called fault finding which is a form of continuous criticism. It's difficult because despite what they have done to me, I have probably done worse to someone else. This has occurred in my personal life with friends and even some family members. My pride has been held over having a progressive relationship that could indeed be a needed blessing in my life. Pride is poison to our souls, and a large form of it comes from arrogance. It simply means caring less about others and more about yourself. With pride and arrogance, we tend to feel as if we have to protect our self-worth. Pride is nothing to be proud of, especially when it has effects on you growing. In today's society, we see this a lot with business partners and also in relationships. Because of an action completed by the other party, we start focusing on the issue and not progressing.

Knowing that we work great in unison, something the other party did could cause everything to fall to crumbles. Some of the best bands and musical groups were broken up because of pride. Pride is shame driven and is one of the seven deadly sins. We must do our best not to practice it, especially when we know deep down what's best for us. Someone would turn down helpful advice or instructions because their pride wouldn't let them open up. We should all strive to progress in our everyday lives and put our human pride on the backburner. In today's society, it's not what you know, but who you know that will take you to the next level. When looking to progress, resources and network are very important. Pride can hinder us from wanting to meet new people, thinking that we can do everything by ourselves. Everyone is looking to be self- made when the truth is that everyone received some type of help from someone, no matter who it was. This a sense of pride is seen as a deadly sin because the first person who helped us was God. With him alone, that should delete any pride out of our hearts. Pride has ruined so many great relationships throughout my life. There were people that have been such blessings to my life and were so good to me but pride got the best of the relationships. We tend to miss out on blessings this way also. No matter what that person did, they most likely have been a blessing in our life, one way or another. Were now blocking God's work when we dismiss a person completely from our lives. I talked earlier on about how I wanted every blessing that was owed to me, and I truly meant it. My pride can indeed cause some of my blessings to disappear because there are times when we must set the environment for the blessings we look to receive.

Owning up to your mistakes may cause the other party to do the same. It could be the first step to overcome pride. Admitting the mistake or apologizing can benefit your personal growth. Just a simple "I'm sorry" goes a long way and can get a relationship back on a progressive path. The next way to overcome pride is to lose all defensiveness. Pride sometimes places us in a place where we are scared to lose favor or status. It causes us to worry about the way the public looks at us and things of that nature. Instead of defending ourselves, we should try to agree and work on the issue. Sometimes the other party's point of view is very much true. We should question and become curious about their point of view. Not taking the criticism personally and looking at it as a growing experience helps a lot also.

Lastly, to overcome our pride, we should practice mindfulness. We should slow down our thought process by accepting and trying to understand those parts of yourself. We can look in the mirror and tell ourselves the truth if no one else knows. We can then activate that mindfulness when we feel pride is taking control of a situation. Take less offense by not viewing everything as a threat but seeing everything as an opportunity to get better. Once we humble ourselves and realize that we can learn from every situation, I believe the process begins to be much easier. Instead of having pride, we can look at the pros of each situation if we didn't let our pride get the best of us. There are places that we all are striving to get to in life that have no place for pride.

We should humble ourselves before God and ask that He remove any traces of this deadly sin and rebuke even the least bit of its attacks. We then will battle pride no more because we will be set free and hold gratitude, knowing that we will forever be moving in a positive direction.

Part 3: The Man
Chapter 20

The process

The process is simple. God's timing, not yours, not your mother's, not your father's but God's timing. I attended a seminar last year, and the speaker said one thing that stuck with me. He said, "God has a pre-written destiny for us. It is a straight line. Ultimately, we make choices that make our path a lot rockier than it should be." A lot of people are in denial, but I believe that the mistakes I made in life had an immediate impact on some events that happened in my life. We have to be accountable for our actions and blame no one else. No matter the influence of peer pressure, we are all our own person. So, when making a mistake, one should step up and say, "It is my fault. "Never say, "If it wasn't for this or that, I would be…" For all of the mistakes I made in life, I take full responsibility. The process always includes a rise, a fall, and a get back. This cycle will repeat itself many times during your life. The main thing is to stay positive during the fall. That is were a lot of people lose faith and give up. Tough times don't last, only tough people do. You have to face a problem head-on with a full pot of steam. Times may get hard, but when down, remember why you started. The door to the room of opportunity swings on the hinges of opposition.

Every day you will be faced with different opposition or resistance from where you plan on going. You must then catch your second wind when the resistance comes. Life is hard, true.

* * *

But not as hard as we sometimes make it seem. They say pressure bust pipes, but honestly, I feel as if it makes you go a tad bit harder. It makes you grind with a sense of purpose. Hustling like it's the first of the month, and the rent is due. I don't know about you, but pressure brings out the best in me. Testing and stretching your grind to the limit. You might be amazed at what some effort along with God can do.

The most important thing to do when you feel pressure is to not panic. The greats were defined by their performances in clutch moments. Those same principles apply to life. It's cool to do it on the regular, but how do you respond when your back is up against the wall? Whenever my back is against the wall, I say a prayer and grind with my head down. When life comes, my advice is to take it on fully with a head full of steam. Facing adversity is a choice that many have a hard time making. There is an old saying that only two things are promised in life, and they are death and pain. But learning to overcome and dealing with situations as they present themselves are keys to life.

Time and time again, I have noticed that adversity brings out the best in me. Never take the "why me" approach during the process. Know that no matter the economic or social status, everyone faces an opposition of some sort. We should look for learning opportunities in every adverse situation. I try to never look at setbacks or loses but only lessons. Prepare for the worst while still praying for the best. Your mindset is everything. How you go into a situation thinking will be a direct reflection on the outcome.

When you are prepared for the worst, it rarely happens, and when it does, you can handle it calmly. We must play chess while the enemy is playing checkers. Think before every action. When deciding, always ask yourself the consequences of the action. Trust the process and believe that the higher power will get you through it all. You should cultivate your courage and faith. These two will help lessen the impact the adversity has on you. Believe and look for the good in every situation. Understand that everything in life has a place and a purpose. Your internal resources should always be important, but another resource which is critical during the process is your external resources. You should have a good support system from maybe family, friends, or both. Someone who will listen to you but also guide you, encourage you, and will hold you accountable for your actions. While listening to the adversity of someone close and sharing experience, it can sometimes feel comforting while going through your battles. I know this from my experiences. When hearing other people's testimony, it reminds me of how good God really is and that he is a faithful God. He hears all and knows all and is working around the clock not only in my life but everyone else's too. This helps me to never take the adversity personal and know that the sun will be out once the stormy weather is over. Remember again that tough times don't last, only tough people do. The next season of ability is dependent on last season's responsibility. We must stay focus and remain calm during the fire.

Chapter 21

Comfort zone

Stepping out on faith and out of your comfort zone is where the magic happens. As I said earlier, to get what we never had, we must do what we have never done. I first heard the term early in my football years and always wondered the real meaning. Football is often called the game of life, and I truly believe this. My coach essentially meant that to get to where we wanted to be, we must do the unordinary and push our bodies to the extreme. Take your body to the limit, and once you get there, go a little bit harder than that. I try to treat life with the same mindset. My biggest fear in life is to be average. So, a lot of the time, I find myself evaluating my life to ensure this

* * *

never happens. This might not be your biggest fear, but to step out of your comfort zone, one must identify the biggest fear and face it head-on. If you are uncomfortable in a familiar place, this is a good thing. Take when I attended college, for example. I could have gone to a college where I knew a lot of people from high school and felt comfortable in the environment. I chose to step out and attend a college in a different state where I knew barely anyone. I was forced to make new friends and make decisions on my own. This kept me out of trouble and could be a direct reflection of the success that I am having to date. Lots of people love their comfort zone because it is easy and simply what they are used to. Some have had the same routine for years, and even though they feel they have more potential to get to the next level, they are

● ● ●
146

afraid of failure. I encourage you to face that fear. Apply for that promotion, start that business, and put yourself first.

God blesses us most when we lean onto Him and not our own understanding. You must think big and act big to gain larger rewards in life. 1 Corinthians 2:9 is one of my favorite Bible verses and really one that sticks close to my heart. The verse says, "But as it is written, Eye hath not seen, nor ear heard, neither have entered into the heart of man, the things which God hath prepared for them that love him." This encourages me to get out of my comfort zone and trust God. Taking risks are also growth experiences, so I feel that everything will be a lesson even if it doesn't go as planned. Life truly begins at the end of your comfort zone. If struggling to know where your comfort zone ends, just think how you would feel if you were in that spot for five years. The comfort zone is home to complacently. It is not essentially a place but more of a state of mind. If you feel that there is no room for improvement or nothing more can be accomplished or achieved, you may be in that comfort zone. You can always do more, learn more, and perfect your craft. A sign to know if you are in your comfort zone is if you are not challenging yourself. This is a self-assessment, and you will be the only one who knows your limits. Another sign you are comfortable is if you lack ambition. You should always dream and be on your toes on how to get to the next level. Obsess yourself with improvement daily. Rejecting change could also be a sign you are in your comfort zone. Change is good and is sometimes needed to stir up the pot. If you are scared to make that move and step out, you are in a comfortable spot. Another indicator of the comfort zone is if you are not learning anything or have the perception that you can't learn anything. Every day is a learning experience. Complacent people get content with what they know and fail to seek new knowledge. The last trait of the comfort zone is feeling stuck or stagnant. If you don't plan to climb out of that state, then you are most likely in a place where you will just adapt to being comfortable. I pray that we all jump off that bridge of fear and step out of our comfort zones. The best things transpire when we are uncomfortable. Challenge yourself daily, become familiar with discomfort, and visualize success. If you can believe it, then you can achieve it. Don't let anything hold you back and step out of that bubble of comfort.

* * *

Chapter 22

The short end of the stick

Growing up, I would always wonder, "Why me?" Early on in my childhood, I began to realize that I seemed to always to have it a little harder than others. As I said earlier, for the most part, I worked hard and expected good things to happen. Because good things happen to good people, right? Not always, I always found myself at the other end of the bargain way too many times, and I began to ask, "Why me?" I was never able to get away with things most people did. Looking back over my life, I'm thankful for the spirit of discipline God instilled in me. It started with things as simple as me getting blamed for things I didn't do as a child and progressed to me even going to jail for something that shouldn't have taken place. I remember as a young child wishing my mom would not be so strict. I would get in trouble for the simplest things while my cousins would not. Sometimes I would get upset at God and look at others' situation and try to compare mine to theirs.

I quickly learned that this was not the way to think. You never know a person's struggle, and it may always look appealing on the outside but may not always be what it seems. I then thought maybe it was bad karma from things my parents did or for times I was disobedient to God. I then still found similar situations, if not worse, once I started my spiritual journey. I wanted to know why God let bad things happen to good people. You might see a person you know who does everything wrong but is still getting blessed in the best way. It never really made sense to me, so I was eager to get to the bottom of it. First of all, I want to say that this was a horrible way to look at life because we should never let our food get cold watching someone else's plate. Soon into my study, I quickly realized why God might allow bad things to happen to his good people. The pain awakens us to God. I have gotten the short end of the stick many times, and many of those times led me to cry out to God. To thirst for him in a way I never would have done without the struggle. I also realized that even though it might not seem so when going through your situation, but these types of things happen to everyone, they just don't always make it public. I can remember times when I was so mad and felt like God was mad at me, but he ended up knowing the best situation to

● ● ●
152

groom me into a better person. I also noticed that bad things happen, but we must alter our attitudes at how we treat the situation. We speak or think things to ourselves and look to prove ourselves right. Positive faith brings salvation and vice versa.

Negative faith brings destruction. Proverbs 23:7 says, "For as a man thinketh in his heart, so is he." The mind is the most powerful tool in our body. Sayings like, "My luck is always bad" or "It figures, this always happens to me" are things we must stop thinking and saying. We are essentially convincing ourselves we are in a horrible vortex. All this does is pull more negativity our way. Mounting the evidence of previous situations doesn't make it true. We should look at facts to oppose the short end by turning the situation around right in the midst of it. Search for ways it can benefit you. The enemy plays tricks on us and wants to convince us that we deserve everything that happens to us. But we must stand up and shout, "Not on God's watch" and recognize the attack is very pivotal. Shifting our mindset into looking for a good thing while in a bad situation is very important. God gives his toughest battles to his strongest soldiers, and we must approach every interaction with the mindset that if he got you to it, he can help you through it.

Chapter 23

Hard work not unnoticed

Growing up, I took pride in working hard at everything that I did. All I knew was hard work from a child. I had been playing tackle football since I was five years old. From peewee to high school, I had always been one of the best athletes on the team. I never had any problems with getting any playing time. It wasn't until high school that I had problems with this issue. In my freshman year, I switched schools in the middle of the summer, so I ended up being the second string running back on the junior varsity team. Being honest with myself, high school was a different level than the little league. I was on the team with people much older than me, and naturally, I was still in the top tier but not the best on the team. The starting running back was also a freshman and a very talented fellow who could cut on the dime and could run a 4.4 on a Sunday morning without stretching. He was said to be the next NFL star out of the city, and everyone knew it. After the JV season was over, he went up to start on varsity as a freshman when their starting running back was injured, and he had a pretty decent playoff game.

Without a doubt, he was clearly a better running back than I was. I was determined to be the best I could be. I was 5' 6'' and ran a 4.7 on my best day. I was obsessed with improvement and began training hard. Sometimes I would train three times a day in a 100-degree weather, trying to sharpen my skills. I was never the biggest, strongest, or fastest on the field, but I was always a playmaker. The next season, I came back better than ever. The other running back didn't really work hard because his God- gifted talent was all he ever needed. My sophomore year, we both went to varsity, and they still favored him over me. He had a great season and began to get early interest from colleges. I felt I was better than him at this point, and after the coaches saw the improvement in me, they altered the lineup to get us both on the field at the same time. He was still the feature back though, and this sometimes made me upset. At this point, it was clear who was better, and I began thinking my hard work was going unnoticed. Then in my 11th-grade year, due to grades, he was unable to play. Even though I was there the whole time, I still was overlooked, and they set out to find another good running back. I was honored to win the hardest working player in the offseason that year, but I wasn't satisfied and still kept working on my craft. Getting bigger, faster, and stronger every day was a difficult task, but I was determined to be the best. I had a pretty good junior year, but my senior year was when I really began to reap the seeds I had been sowing. I worked that off season like never before. I ended up getting a part- time job at Sears in my local mall and had to take two buses to get to practice on time.

Discipline, hard work, and dedication was the only way I was able to take this on. Grinding every day with my head down, others began to take notice. He was now back and coming to reclaim his spot as the feature running back. This was also his senior year. Remembering he had always been better than me, he thought it would be a piece of cake. I remember him telling me one day that I might as well transfer because there was no way that I would play over him. But as training camp progressed, I had a chip on my shoulder. I knew from my hard work that without any doubt, I was better than him. He was relying on the same talent he had four years ago, but I had been crafting and working on my game every day. I rarely ever took a day off, so I was essentially three years better than I was my freshman year. Hard work beats talent when talent doesn't work hard. This is not a myth but a fact. When you mix talent with hard work, it becomes a scary combination. I went on to lead the team in rushing, surpassing 1,000 yards while sharing carries with him. I went on

* * *

to win Player of the Year and also received a scholarship while he unfortunately received nothing. Along that journey, I would be lying if I told you I didn't think about giving up and even transferring when he told me I should. It can get very tough, and you might think the hard work is going in vain. I think back to times in college. I would head out to do drills at midnight because I wanted it that bad. I began to think that it was all for no reason when I quit playing football. But now in life, I am starting to receive the benefits of all that hard work despite it being in other fields of life. I can assure you that someone is paying attention, especially the man above who knows all and sees all.

When I would get tired of working hard, I referred back to Galatians 6:9 where it says, "So let's not get tired of doing what is good. At just the right time, we will reap a harvest of blessing if we don't give up." Keep the faith and hold on. To shine hard, you must grind hard and remember that it is always on God's timing and not our own. Patience goes hand in hand with hard work. What you plant today might not blossom tomorrow. It takes time to build anything worth substance and value. As long as you keep the faith and keep building, he will shine his light on you.

Chapter 24

Success leaves clues

I often hear people speaking of success as if it is some secret mystery formula. The truth is, success is more like a simple addition problem when most think it's some erratic quadratic equation. Success is easier than it sounds. I often have people ask me how I got to the point I am at today. Before you pay for some crazy seminar to figure out someone's secret to success, remember that you heard it here first. Success is free and much simpler than everyone thinks. Lots of people think that successful people did some big drastic thing that enabled them to make it. When the truth is that all they did was do that same tedious steps, you chose not to do

● ● ●
162

every day. I am a person who seems to feel uneasy when I have no task to complete. I tend to feel like I'm wasting my time.

When I graduated from college and went on to work in Corporate America is when I began to see the traces. There was no dress code for my job, but for some reason, I would wake up every day and put on a dress shirt and pants. I can recall my manager asking jokingly, "Have you applied for another job?" I am a firm believer in acting like the person you strive to be and not the person you are today. I even recall a team member saying that I dressed as if I was the CEO. It was going right over their heads, and these are all Aerospace Engineers we are talking about. I was a CEO. Well, in my head I was, they just didn't know it yet. To be completely honest with you, I didn't either.

● ● ●

Many people were attracted to the position I held because of the flexibility in the schedule. We basically could come in any time from 6 to 10 AM as long as we completed our nine hours total for a complete workday. At first, I began showing up to work at 7:00 AM and feeling good because everyone else showed up at around 9:30 AM. But for some odd reason, I felt like I was selling myself short still. I had to realize that even though I was being praised for coming in that early, that wasn't early to me at all. I was fresh out of college where we had to be in workouts, dressed, and ready at 5:45 AM. So, I changed my start time to 6 AM to better fit my mental obedience. Little did I know that by doing this, the amount of productive activity I could accomplish day today would be nothing short of amazing. I was able to get off, take a nap, work out,

● ● ●

work on my business and do homework for graduate school. I remember one of my co-workers telling me, "Man, you act like you own the place." At first, I would laugh and not take it seriously until one day it clicked in my head. These traits were the reason I was becoming successful. I soon found out that my job had a tuition reimbursement. They would pay for your master's degree immediately. It sounded like everyone would take advantage of this opportunity, right? So, I set out to find a co-worker who would like to enroll in the courses with me.

This sounded like an easy task, but I was sadly mistaken and was unable to find anyone willing to take the courses with me. Lots of people mentioned how they would start in a couple of years or how they were tired of school. This really confused me because these were all engineers we were

* * *

talking about. I remember trying to figure this out and realized that success was not always monetary. Money was not a tool to measure someone's success by. These extraordinary traits to everyone else were just a part of my everyday tasks. I didn't even see them as anything special because they were things I had gotten used to doing. I would watch motivational videos of billionaires and millionaires to see how they accumulated their wealth. Again, I began to think, "Man, it had to be something else they weren't sharing because these are the same things that are happening daily in my life." Praying, working hard, focusing on the small things, staying humble, and giving God all the glory. Success is not some secret crabby patty formula. After doing a study on the traits of the most successful people in the world, I figured out that almost everyone

* * *

around them knew their potential years before they became who they are today. We tend to look at where people are today and think that they all had overnight success. No matter what social media portrays of people, we never see their detailed background story and what they did every day to reach their peak. If you look to be successful, I would suggest focusing on those clues consistently. Doing the things everyone else dreads doing and doing them effortless is key. Do them wholeheartedly and make them a part of your everyday life. Look to act as if you are the person you dreamt of becoming today. You will eventually look up in the mirror and see a shell of your former self. Embrace the differential approach in doing the things people are too lazy to consistently do. That hard and rugged road to success is indeed difficult, but it is not impossible to attain. Practice the same clues talked about earlier day to day, and you will soon see yourself setting the tone for greatness. The formula for success is simply explained as greatness daily multiplied by consistency.

Chapter 25

Purposed Living

Life may not be tied with a bow, but it is indeed a gift. Although we sometimes forget while being overwhelmed with the hills and valleys of day to day life, we must not forget it's a blessing to be here. This was something I too often took for granted. It wasn't until people whom I had grown up with started leaving off the face of the earth. These days I am happy to just open my eyes and see another day. But it wasn't until I found out my purpose that I began to strive and enjoy life. Living without purpose is like running a race with no finish line. Nothing gives a person peace like a sound understanding of where they are going. Everyone was born with a talent, and you

* * *

are in control of bringing that talent out through your purpose.

When looking for your purpose, it will be the thing you do the absolute best with the least amount of effort. Those were my passions and things other people were telling me that I should be doing. Although similar in definition, they are very different but can indeed be tied together once you've found your passion. Your passion can indeed be something to thrive in, but it is something that you must work hard to do and be driven by your feelings to be great. Your purpose is the reason why you do something. When you find your purpose and attack it with passion, you become dangerous. I can recall times before I found out my purpose. I was always upset because I wasn't where I thought I should be in life. But now, I realize the reasons why God didn't allow me to excel in those areas because that was not my purpose.

Chapter 26

Journey Lee

May 5,2018, at 9:23 AM, God blessed me with the best gift known to man. A beautiful, healthy baby girl. My life was on the uphill because I chose to make a change for the better. It's a feeling that I can't explain. A feeling of someone depending on you. Someone so innocent and that doesn't deserve any excuses. When I found out my daughter's mother was pregnant, it was like a fire ignited under my behind. The life I was used to living would soon have to come to an end. To be a great father, I would have to do almost a full 360. I would have to discipline myself and hold myself accountable for every action. This was when I began to really walk with Christ during my journey.

⚬ ⚬ ⚬

I immediately joined a church near my college and dove into the word. I met a guy named Reverend Odom, who changed my life. He prayed with me when I was at some very low points, and I have the ultimate respect for him still to this day. I gave everything to the Lord, and at that point is where the magic began to happen. From that point forward, I made up my mind to do what I needed to do, and I did it. I had applied for so many jobs, but I hadn't gotten any calls back. Almost suddenly, I found myself with two jobs that were almost an hour away from school. It was fine though, because like I told you, I was determined to do anything for my daughter. Then on my first day at the job, my engine blew. So now I found myself with two jobs and no way to get there. I had to work seven days a week and had no time to even go to church. I then made the ultimate sacrifice. I began going to early morning service at 7:30 a.m. on Sundays and then to both of my jobs.

It was one of the best sacrifices I have made thus far. It looked like everything was crumbling right before my eyes, but I had to keep the faith for Journey Lee. My obedience was definitely noted by the one above. I always made it to work, and I know there's no one to blame but God. She gave me a drive like nothing had ever given me before. I even had bad news when it came to my graduation in a few months. I needed to retake a class that I had failed. Because of this, I was forced to take 18 hours at my college and 6 hours online at another college in the same semester. This sounds almost crazy, but like I said, I had no choice but to go hard to accommodate the extreme

* * *

circumstances. Twenty-four hours in one semester is uncommon. The funny thing is, that was my best semester in school. A full course load, two full-time job, still that was no excuse. My daughter didn't know anything and was innocent. This is the mindset I took on. She didn't ask to be here, and for that, she can't suffer for my irresponsibility.

I remember praying to the Lord that I would be able to take care of her without the help of anyone. To do this, I did one of the hardest things I ever had to do in life. I had to walk away from my first love – the game of football. I had to wake up and smell the coffee. Doing this allowed me to focus on my studies and get on the job hunt. I remember getting off from work at 10 PM and staying in the student library until they closed at midnight. I remember being forced

• • •
175

out for trying to finish one more job application. God answered my prayers when he blessed me with an aerospace engineering position which I was not qualified for. When my daughter's mother found out she was pregnant, I was probably at one of the lowest points in my life, but that essentially made me a man.

For the first time, I put myself second and put someone else first. Now looking back at the situation, I have no doubt I could've been dead or in jail if not for her. I owe my daughter the world because she changed my life, little does she know. I owe her the world, and through the grace of God, I will give it to her.

Chapter 27

It could've been me

Growing older, you start to see certain things. When I was young, I used to see homeless people, and my mom would tell me how they used to be so cool in school and class growing up. Seeing this is why I never laugh at someone who isn't doing well because I know people who have been in those shoes personally. I even have had family members who used to be successful that were now out on the streets, but it still never registered. What went wrong, what did they do to deserve such a thing? A series of unfortunate events may be led to many people, but with some people, it was a very thin line. A lot of people look down on homeless people or feel better than them. I

• • •

have the mentality of treating the janitor with the same respect as the CEO. This follows suit with treating a millionaire just how you would treat a person on the street. The same respect should be given to all of God's people.

It took for me to witness people that I know ending up in that place and even ending up homeless myself to know that there is a very thin line, and if you don't remain humble, you too could be there. It could happen much easier than you think. I remember it like it was yesterday. I went from being the starting running back at a division one football program to being homeless thousands of miles away from home and without a scholarship. I wondered what went wrong, what did I do? I was still praying. Where was the line that I had crossed?

I realized it was very slim between me being where I was and having nowhere to live. I thank God for my daughter's mother because without her, I could have been out on the streets too. The same thing situation can be applied to life in general. We are blessed to wake up every morning, and a lot of time, we tend to take this for granted. We have this sort of mindset that we have our whole life to live, and we can get our lives together when we get old. Sad to say, but in this day and age, you never know. I would rather stay ready so that I don't have to get ready. I have had lots of family members who I loved dearly go on to be with the Lord. It was when my younger sister's brother on her father's side, who was the same age as me left that it hit me. You never know when your time will come. His sins were no worse than my sins, and that's what

* * *

scares me the most. When the good die young, it is an eye- opener every time. Where did they go wrong? I feel that even If they were doing something wrong, I had been down that path before as well. It took for them to lower one of my best friends in a casket for it to really hit home. He was a successful entrepreneur who had graduated college with honors about three weeks before he was gunned down for something he had nothing to do with. That's when I realized it could have been me. I vowed to myself after that day that I would try my best to take no day for granted in all aspects of life. I sometimes find myself very thankful for the simple things such as for my daughter being healthy, for the food I eat, even for my legs and being able to walk.

(Picture of some childhood friends and I carrying our fellow

friend Herbert's casket to his grave)

Chapter 28

They say I'm a role model

A couple of years ago, one of my good friends who was working at our high school asked me to speak to his students. I thought to myself, "Man, I'm no role model. Why would he ask me to do this?" Then soon after that, an old teacher asked me to speak to his students. In both situations, I pondered and thought of why they wanted me to talk to these kids. Knowing all the things I have done wrong, I never wanted them to look up to me. This was before my real journey with Christ ever started. At the time, I didn't really know why Jesus died. I would sometimes ask what I had done to deserve this type of favor. Why did I make it out of the hood and not the person who

* * *

had all the promise? I remember always feeling like an average joe and being regular while growing up. Even when I set out to work harder than everyone else, I still sometimes would be in the shadow of some of my peers. So, at this point in my life, a serious question I asked was, "Why would God choose me to be the role model?" I happened to find my way into church one Sunday while my pastor was preaching out of the book of Amos. Amos was a man who was not a professional prophet, nor was he the son of a prophet. I see myself in the same shoes. I was the son of a man who did not graduate from high school and a single mother who had gone to the military. Why was I blessed to go on and receive a bachelors, and better yet, a master's degree? I have friends with married parents who hold college degrees but didn't finish

* * *

high school. I can name ten people, or more who I believe are worthier than I am to be in my position today. The pastor went on to speak about how Amos was a man with no credential but with a calling. As he went on with the story, he emphasized how God loves to use a common man to do his work.

Everyone he uses is flawed and imperfect in his eyes. He uses ordinary people in many situations to do extraordinary things so that he alone can receive all the glory. Many people were golden children growing up, and people knew even back then they would be something great. I would expect those people to be called role models and the people to look up to. When those people go on to do great things, God may get overlooked because that was sort of expected of them. But when he uses a diamond in the ruff, it would encourage similar people that come from similar situations that they can do it too. For instance, if a guy who had a father who was in the NFL and was always the top football player in his class grows to be a millionaire by being selected as a top NFL draft pick, God will indeed receive some glory. But it's a different kind of glory if the boy who made it out the projects grows up to be a millionaire through the technology field. When the project kid tells that it was God, people would have a certain type of feeling to be motivated, thinking that if he made it from this place, I can too. Then it all made sense why God was making me a role model when I wasn't even trying to be. He was using me as a living testimony for the kids in my neighborhood that they too can make it out with his help. Even after all the things I had done wrong, just the simple fact of me

* * *

overcoming adversity and graduating from college was something those young kids could learn. That will teach them how to face the adversity when it's their time to face it. God places us in certain situations to better the lives of other individuals. I now know that the reasons why I receive certain blessings is for that exact reason. We must share it with the younger generation because they need it. He died for our sins, so we should never not feel worthy to be a role model or do his work.

Chapter 29

Hustle & Pray

I know hustlers, and I know prayer warriors. The hustlers hustle, and the prayer warriors pray. Some try to hustle around the clock and don't believe in sleep. Some try to pray for a situation and wait on God to make something shake. In the KJV, James 2:17 says: "Even so faith, if it hath not works, is dead, being alone." This should be emphasized in the lives of even the best prayer warriors. Perhaps the MSG version of James 2:17 makes it a lot clearer by saying, "Dear friends, do you think you'll get anywhere in this if you learn all the right words but never do anything?" Does merely talking about faith indicate that a person has it? For instance, you come upon an old

● ● ●

friend dressed in rags and half-starved and say, "Good morning, friend! Be clothed in Christ! Be filled with the Holy Spirit!" And then you walk off without providing so much as a coat or a cup of soup. Where does that get you? Isn't it obvious that God- talk without God-acts is outrageous nonsense? Then we have the hustlers that says that if you don't hustle, you don't eat. This motivates many, but I see this as having little faith because the Bible says, Look at the birds. They don't plant or harvest or store food in barns, for your heavenly Father feeds them. And aren't you far more valuable to him than they are?

Plies had a song called "I'm in love with money. "He rapped that he grinds twenty hours and sleeps for four. I love the concept, but I don't agree with it completely. You can love the hustle and love the grind, but there's only so much we can do on our own. We need God. We must hold strong to our faith because it is the very thing that leads us towards the things we hope for. It's the thing that keeps us moving forward, even if that movement seems slow and uneventful. Why? Because like we said, faith without work is dead. Faith is designed to always spur us on to obedience in Christ and to ultimately be like him. It is the evidence of things we do not see. Hustle and prayer merged together are the recipe to success, I believe. They are each very powerful in their own regards but can be very dangerous in a good way when together. Pride yourself in being the type to say a prayer first before going out and putting a hustling effort toward whatever it is that you just prayed for. By no means am I telling you not to hustle, but what I am saying is that you must pray harder. The hustle brings the dollar, the prayer brings the knowledge., and the persistence brings success.

Take the wheel

Sometimes I find myself hustling and
praying and hustling and praying but still
find myself in a place and feeling like I have
not done enough. I wonder if I'm not
praying the right prayer or if I am not going
hard enough. I concluded that I couldn't do
it all alone, and I had to let Him take the
wheel. When he meets us there, he can take
us to unthinkable places. We tend to put a
cap on his power, but time and time again, I
see that I have no clue of the real power. We
tend to think to take the God street not
knowing that he is a God of avenues.
Avenues are everlasting when streets tend to
always take an end. We must also remember
that God only funds his ideas. I have been

practicing asking him for guidance, even when completing the simplest task. When must always take the backseat approach. I remember times in my early childhood when we would ride around, and I would ask my mother where we were headed. She would reply by saying, "just ride and don't worry about where we are going." I used to think she was being very mean at the time, but now when I look back on it, she was teaching me a life lesson. Control what you can control, and needless to say, things are completely out of our control most of the time. This is an uncomfortable spot to be in, but sometimes it's the best spot to be in. A lot of times, our human nature will cause us to crash out if we were driving. We think on emotions and wants while he thinks through his will and needs. We should wake up daily with the mindset of not knowing what will

* * *

happen but with reconciliation that it will be good. This uncomfortable state is pretty difficult to be in, but we must become comfortable with being uncomfortable. This starts to happen when we ride shotgun with God. You find yourself doing things you never thought you could accomplish or going places you never thought you could go. When allowing him to handle everything, I found myself feeling out of place in the places I used to be a regular at. I wasn't uneasy because of the people but more because of who I was becoming. I was a different person than who I used to be. The quickest way to lose focus on your future is to keep going back to your past. When we give control to him, we have no worries because he makes us a shell of our old selves. I can remember being dead broke and trying to hustle like no other. In six months, I had learned and mastered stocks, learned drop shipping on Amazon, and became very knowledgeable in real estate. I completed neither of these tasks simultaneously.

It was always in the form of "okay, this is not working for me, so let me try the next hustle." I was praying, but the truth is I was trying to outwork God. I was going from a 9-hour shift to taking a 20- minute nap and staying up all night while doing real estate task or studying stocks. I sacrificed my prayer time and thought that it would all pay off. Boy was I wrong. I found little to no success in each of these areas that I was very affluent in. I had watched every YouTube video on real estate, and I was very active in the trading group. But nothing was clicking. I asked God what it was he wanted me to do, and he said, "surrender it all to me." I stopped trying to do all the work and asked him to meet me right where I was. And boy oh boy, he wasted no time. Opportunity after opportunity began to unfold in my life, and I had no doubt who was behind the success. People began to tell me they admired how hard I was going in my respected areas, and I always made sure to tell them I don't deserve any of the glory. It's all God. When he took the wheel, he took me to a place in life that I thought would be impossible to reach. With peace, happiness, and relationships. I then began to see that even all those skills I learned while trying to do it alone began to play a part in my daily life. He was preparing me for the next level, and here I was trying to figure out a word that had no definition. I say all of this to tell you that it's okay to hustle and pray, but it will be a lot easier if you hustle, pray, then let God take the wheel.

* * *

Chapter 31

If you know, you know

To whom much is given, much is required. He who is qualified must go through the fire. If you know better, you must do better and will be held accountable for your actions. 1 Corinthians 13:11 says, "When I was a child, I spoke as a child, I understood as a child, I thought as a child; but when I became a man, I put away childish things." We must hold ourselves liable and assure that we do what is required to maintain our blessings. When you have a purpose and a calling on your life, more is required of you than the average human being. We are not allowed to take the easy way out like most people. A close friend of mine, and I always joke about how God will never let us get anything too easy. And the truth is we appreciate every blessing much more because of this. God rewards us for good works and punishes us for bad works. I used to wonder why a certain individual got away with doing something bad because as soon as I did it, there were horrible consequences. Whether it be from my parents or God himself, I was never able to stray too far away. When I was broke, I used to wonder how a lot of my friends could make fast money so easily. But as soon as I attempted to take the easy way out, I would find myself in a bad situation. Then I thought back to the things my parents instilled in me as a child. I definitely knew right from wrong at an early age. Because of this, I was held responsible ever since. This is not the case with everyone. We can't compare the next person's life to ours. Despite their age, some people may

* * *

not know right from wrong. They are not subject to the standards that we are. I was never able to recognize why I was always chastised for my actions, and honestly, it was hard to understand. As I have begun to flourish in my adult life, I know the reason why I was never able to get away.

Those acts did not line up with my destiny, and I have no doubt that's the reason why God blocked it. Even when He allowed me to stray off the path, I was always able to find my way back before I went too far into the deep end. He had a life full of magnificent things waiting for me, but I chose to be disobedient. He required discipline on my part because of the places he would take me to later to life. I realized that I was never able to do those things that other people did because if charged with even one of those serious crimes, my life would've been ruined. I can recall a time when I was doing wrong and got a call out of the blue from a close friend. He had told me he had a dream that I was shipped off to prison right before my college graduation. When I was doing wrong, that was my worst fear. I had been having nightmares about this same circumstance. There are so many situations I can recall that I should have been caught but wasn't due to some crazy circumstance. I began to think I was just slick and lucky. When In reality, God was showing me favor even when I had given up on him. I used to find myself mad that all the fast money plans I would come up with never worked out as planned. Even when collaborating with seasoned criminals, it never went all the way right when I was involved. We used to just think that I had bad luck when, in reality,

* * *

I was really blessed. Some of those same friends or associates that were doing those things back then are either six feet under or in the state penitentiary. He had already known who I would ultimately become, and I was covered even when I wasn't living right. I finally realized living right went much smoother. Sowing good seeds is something very overlooked in this game of life. Everything now seems to work for my good no matter the situation. I began to not be blinded by desires of the flesh. On my journey with Christ, I realized that what he would have for me in the future would be worth my obedience. When doing bad, I always was punished, and when doing good, I was rewarded. Bad energy is something that can hover over you when not living right. Especially when you know right from wrong it will

come down the worst. We must set the
environment for our blessings my sowing
good seeds. If not, those wonderful blessing
can indeed slip away, but the good
thing is it's never too late to start setting the
environment. I realized, and I am now very
thankful for the discipline he set on my life.
Without that self-control he made me
develop I couldn't imagine where I would be
today.

Chapter 32

1%

I often hear people talk about how 20% of people are successful, while the other 80% of the population struggle with the concept. I believe in this theory that the individuals in the 20% are making large amounts of commitment and sacrifice to achieve success in their lives. This is true, but while many try to make it into the 20%, I have had my sight set on the 1%. The margin of error between the 20% and the 1% seems like a lot, but the margin is pretty slim. Very successful individuals are a part of this 20%, but few are willing to take it to the next level. Extreme focus in a couple key areas could eliminate that 19%. Consistency plays a big role in succeeding. Consistency is defined as acting or doing the same task the same way over time, especially so as to be fair or accurate. Doing the same thing over and over with quality is what sets you apart. That is something that 99% of people do not do. To get what you never had, you have to do what you've never done.1% of people are extremely successful, and they have some key traits that I am going to address. The first trait I believe is having faith.

Believing in something bigger than yourself. No matter what race or religion, faith is key. Faith is the evidence of things not seen. Having faith in yourself and a higher power, doing right by others, and knowing that you didn't do it by yourself is more important than any rules and regulations of religion.

Setting goals and being successful also go hand in hand. Most people don't set goals because they don't think it is worth the time. But the reality is that setting goals help align your actions. A goal is merely a dream with a deadline. You should look at your goals multiple times a day to assure you are taking the steps necessary to accomplish them on a daily basis. There are different types of goals, but I prefer a list of long and also short-term goals.

People who set goals are more productive and tend to have better focused efforts. Setting goals is a very underrated task and helps you think about what you want to accomplish and why. Reading is another key trait in successful individuals. In today's society, reading has taken a backseat. Especially in the black community, we do little to no reading. A wise man once told me that if they wanted to keep a secret from a black man that they would put it in a book.

The brightest people are always learning, and you can never obtain too much knowledge. Reading is a necessity, but people always make up excuses of why they don't read. Maybe it's that they don't have enough time or don't have the attention span. In this day and age, there are alternatives for almost any excuse that you have for not reading. Excuses are monuments of nothingness that build bridges to nowhere. Those who use these tools of incompetence are masters of nothingness. Therefore, there are no excuses for not reading. Instead of making excuses, the most successful people prioritize their personal learning. The next trait of successful people is the ability to constantly adapt. Times are constantly changing day to day. What worked yesterday will not always work tomorrow. If you can't see how much you have grown in a span of six months then you might not be growing fast enough. Adapting goes hand in hand with personal learning. Never become satisfied and always thrive to be on top of your game. You should never have barriers and always be willing to change yourself to be better and more productive. Embracing the ambiguity is another important factor in shrinking the 1%.

Your path might not be quite clear, but the top 1% love this. They love taking risks and making challenging decisions. This allows for them to become creative and stand out from the competition. The harder the decision and risk essentially mean, the higher the impact and reward could be. Staying healthy is one point that is looked over in slimming the 1%. Your health can directly reflect your wealth. Staying energetic and attacking each day energetically is very important. What you put into your body and exercise are some decisions to consider. You should take care of your body and hygiene to catapult your success. Networking and taking pride in relationships is critical. We live in a world today of not what you know but who you know can change your life. You should make great business relationships because they can indeed lead to great opportunities. Also, always follow up when networking because it could always be an opportunity to create meaningful relationships with a likeminded person. Holding yourself accountable is something that must be done also. Take responsibility for all of your actions and never blame others. Not taking accountability for your actions could ultimately prevent your personal growth and develop you a bad reputation. Surround yourself with others with the same mindset. The doctors hang with doctors' concept is always in affect. I try to only hang around others who can motivate and propel me on my success ladder. No matter family or friends, sometimes taking a step back to further your dreams without offending others is sometimes challenging.

Energy is everything and should be never taken for granted. The last and most vital success trait is knowing how to fight through adversity. Playing football and just defeating the odds of where I come from, helped me a lot with this. Most people have never had anything drastic happen to them in their lives. So, when an unfortunate event occurs, they tend to get knocked off their pivot. Nothing is wrong with getting knocked off, but it's how fast and if you get up is what is most important. We should never let our circumstances affect our vision. Keep our head clear and focused on the goal even through hard times. It is easy to focus when everything is kosher. But when adversity strikes is ultimately what determines your character. The 1% is a slim and elite club to be a part of. It may seem unattainable, but by following these cardinal steps, you might find yourself there on accident.

Chapter 33

Good Vibes Only

You attract the energy that you give off. Spread Good Vibes, think positively, and enjoy Life. It's as easy as it sounds right? We make it much more complicated than it really has to be, but that's the human nature of it all. Dealing with negativity can be a downer on your own life. Happiness starts within and not based on external situations. For me and my friend's good vibes only is not just a saying but a way of life. We pride ourselves in always being in a good mood and protecting our peace. Some could think back of a time where our parents had gotten off of work and came home with an attitude. Even then, that could stir the mood in the household for the rest of the evening.

* * *

As I have approached my early adult life, I see now why our parents might have been upset. But this doesn't negate the fact that they were spreading bad energy without noticing it. Facing trials and tribulations throughout my journey up until this point has been a huge obstacle. Part of my doing though, was never letting energy sway on me too hard. Not to say that we won't get angry because we are human beings with feelings at the same time.

My mom would always tell me as a child that when you are angry, you can't seem to do anything right. I pondered on this statement and concluded when approaching a situation with negative energy you can't focus on the task at hand while dwelling on the energy that upset you. The moral is to set and enforce limits to the energy surrounding others and even yourself. Never allow others pity party to recruit you. No problem with listening but listen to encourage without listening to join. Everyone has that coworker or teammate who is always complaining. Next time they complain, try to negate their negative energy with opposing energy. Know when to distance yourself when necessary. It's kind of like second hand smoke with you getting more damage to your space than them. Misery loves company, and we must protect good energy with a first line of defense. Sometimes it might be you with the bad energy without noticing. Try to always see the good in every situation. This is how I deal with bad energy too because it is natural. Life and death is in the power of the tongue, according to Proverbs 18:21.

You can speak your way too or through anything. Another way to spread good vibes is to focus on solutions and not the problem. If we wanted to, we could complain 24/7 about any and everything. Anytime someone asks me how I am doing, I reply with, "I can't complain." A lot of replies to that statement are people saying right because at the end of the day no one cares anyways. I stand on this. No reason to complain because not diming your problem down but everyone is facing their own battles in life. Where you focus your attention directly reflects your emotional state. Shifting your focus toward actions that can improve the circumstance is important. Responding without reacting could take a lot of stress away from a situation. After hearing bad news or interacting in a situation that will take you out of character. Simply take a

breath and think what Jesus would do.
Depending on the situation, this can lighten
the vibe of a very tense situation.

Chapter 34

5P's

Stay ready so you don't have to get ready. A principle that I have lived by for quite some time now. You never know when opportunity will come, but when it does the worst feeling in the world is when you are not ready. Proper preparation prevents poor performance. The opportunities can come from anywhere, and lots of things in life happen when we least expect it. We must always have a for a rainy-day state of mind. Whether that be with finances, school, work, or just life in general. When preparing properly, you can make yourself ready for almost anything that life throws at you. This is the mindset we must take on.

Waiting for a lucky break while not

prepared can cause you to panic when the situation presents itself. I can remember being in high school, making my mind up that I wanted to play football on the next level. I remember waking up 2 hours before school started doing abs and footwork drills.

After getting to school, I worked out again, and after school one more time. Me doing this everyday became something I did on the regular. I didn't notice at the time, but I was preparing myself for college football and ideally for the rest of my life. I didn't know how or who would give me a scholarship but whatever university I attended they would get one of the hardest working players in the country. Little did I know shortly after I would indeed receive a scholarship and have workouts at 5:15 in the mornings daily. While the other freshmen struggled to adapt with waking up early and working out, I was up bright eyed and ready to roll. But this probably wouldn't have been the case if I had not been used to doing this all those mornings in high school. Now working in Corporate America, veterans of the job question how I come in before 6 a.m. bright eyed and ready to work. Many people say they have tried it for a while, but it didn't work for them. Little did they know it has been my lifestyle for over 10 years now.

Proper preparation is muscle memory. It is said that it takes 21 days to form a habit and 90 days to build a lifetime. Every day we should wake up sharp and aware of life. We should focus daily on everything we want in life and the steps we can take to achieve it. I don't have many fears but not living up to my potential and missing out on blessings

* * *

are honestly some that I struggle with. Seizing opportunity and winning every day is something I live by. The small things most definitely matter when you study the lives of the most successful people. You will begin to realize that it's not really anything they do that's very extravagant. They just do the small things right consistently. The all-time greats in sports are the ones who took pride in practice. I hear stories all the times of Kobe Bryant, Lebron James, Tom Brady, Floyd Mayweather, and Michael Jordan and how they all prepared for competition. Every player who has ever played with Kobe's speaks about his insane practice habits. There is no doubt in my mind that those long practices correlate directly to his 20-year successful career. I even sometimes substitute the second "P" while keeping the

same concept of work without faith is dead.
It now becomes proper prayer prevents poor
performance. Always prepare for the worst
while praying for the best. Applying to these
two concepts to your life is almost like
having a cheat code for success. No matter
what comes up, you will be ready for it
through your preparation and prayer.

Chapter 35

Don't sell out

Good, Better, Best. Why be good when you can be great? We all have dreams, and I want to ensure you that it is ok to chase them. We should never sell ourselves short for any reason. We are selling out million-dollar minds for a yearly salary because it is safe. I am not against education in any way, shape, or form. I have enjoyed and learned many things all throughout my life up until this point of completing my post-secondary degree. Lots of the material learned throughout my studies I feel was busy work. You too probably can remember times throughout grade school and high school thinking there is no way this could translate to real life. Not dimming the light on courses like english literature or even high-level mathematics courses. There should be more emphasis on classes taught about real estate, investing, and financial literacy. This is why many students graduate and their education can't translate to the real world. I feel strongly that society helps us in selling ourselves short. We are living in a space that will approve an 18-year- old for a $250,000-student loan but not a $15,000 business loan. After completing college and pondering to my self is that all this education has taught me was to be an employee. People always stress that you must go to school, get an education, so you can get a good job. But why not go to school and get educated so you can give out jobs. You may hear me talk about mindset a lot because I feel it is one of the most important tools in life. How can I be something that I was not raised to be? I thought that once I graduated and got a good job, I would feel like I was done, and I had won if life. Although I could have let the pats on the back get to my head and feel like I had made it, it just didn't feel right. After talking with my mother, and she informed me that some of her coworkers said that I had received their dream job and that I should be thankful. I told her that I did feel blessed, but that I felt like it was more to life than this. She mistook this for me being ungrateful. I had to explain to her that I was indeed was not doubting this blessing, but I felt as if it were a footstool instead of a podium. Lots of people feel accomplished and forget the goals they set out years ago. Work life balance is a must. While I find nothing wrong with a company, I feel we as people must also put ourselves first and not sell out to anything handicapping us from greatness. We are essentially working for another person's dreams, so I feel why shouldn't we be able to work on ours. Selling yourself short is saying I will not work on my dreams and goals because I am too tired when I get home from work. This cycle will repeat, and before we know it, life happens, and our dreams and wishes are a thing of the past. To give a company's goals 40 hours a week and your own goals zero hours make no sense to me. I want everything owed to me in life nothing more and nothing less, every blessing that the man above has for me, I want to be in a position to attain it. Selling out and taking the safe route can indeed prevent us from those blessings. TRAP is an acronym that I keep close to my heart. It means to take risks and prosper. Reading the story of Steve Harvey is a prime example of how taking risks and not selling out could result in. In a world that is changing so quickly, I believe the only strategy that is guaranteed to fail is not taking risks.

Chapter 36

Time

Time is the indefinite continued progress of existence and events in the past, present, and future. It is measured in hours, minutes, and seconds. There are 24 hours in a day, 1,440 minutes in a day, and 86,400 seconds in a day. Once it passes, we will never get it back. Despite those large numbers we have to take full advantage of our time. We take time for granted more than anything else. My philosophy is simple, I look to maximize the time I have in a day every day. Anything lost can be found again except for time wasted. To be all we can be and maximize our day we can't disrespect time. I would define disrespecting time as doing things that serve no purpose in the betterment of your day. Pointless tasks that will not take me to the level I look to reach have been taken away from my schedule. This helps with limiting the distractions that we have in a day. Before I started respecting my time, I found myself never accomplishing goals that had been set. Planning is very essential to this. Simply just setting a small outline or schedule to keep your day aligned with your goals could be something very vital. We must also limit and take control of our own time.

We can't allow others to dictate our time. It's okay to put yourself first and tell someone else no. There is power in the word no. When you say yes to something, you are saying no to all the things you could have been doing. I realized quite some time ago that I was really distracted by the television.

* * *

So, I disconnected my cable just to see how would impact my time in a day. Needless to say, I've seen a drastic change in my life. I went from not having enough time to having too much time in a day. Juggling a full-time job, full course load, and multiple side hustles can seem quite overwhelming. But when I decided to maximize my time, I saw myself being a lot more productive in my day to day life. Control your time, and don't let the time control you. We are the author of our lives and dictate what can go on. I would even still have time left over after completing all of these tasks. Time is precious and should always be seen in that manner. We all have the same 24 hours, and what we do with it directly impacts the type of life you live or desire to live.

Chapter 37

Down but not out

Just when I thought I had made it I was faced with yet another blow to the face. About a month before graduating from graduate school I with faced with one of my most difficult challenges. I know you have heard me say that a lot but honestly, it's as if the previous struggle preps me for the next one. It reminded me of an old Mario game. When you had made it past the final level you had the ultimate face off with Bowser to win the game. I was charged with a ridiculous charge by someone who had once been very close to me. I had been betrayed in the worst way and hung out to dry. I had said earlier in the text that I had been to jail, and I wasn't going back. However, facing this situation and it was looking like that

* * *

was right where I would end up. I was scheduled to catch a flight to propose to my then girlfriend in the coming days. I had spoken with my lawyer and we agreed on a set time for me to show up to see the judge, so a bond could be set. However, there was a misunderstanding and I arrived long before her. I had essentially come there and turned myself in. I had no bond company with me nor was my lawyer there. I had seen a guy on the docket and he whispered to me that my lawyer should hurry because they were going to book me into the county jail if she didn't show up. He eased out of the courtroom to find my then girlfriend to tell her the news. The lawyer was in a completely different case at the time and hurried over. She got there in a couple minutes and approached the judge. My girlfriend was told that she had about 15 minutes to find a bail bondsman or I would be booked and probably have to spend the

* * *

next few days behind bars.

I had a flight to catch the next morning to propose to her and she had no clue. It had to be God because within those fifteen minutes she had found a bails bondsman that was about $500 dollars cheaper than any of the others and they just so happened to be across the street from the courthouse. I was out of custody in about 30 minutes and on my way. In the following days I would propose, and she said yes. God blocked every attempt of the enemy just as he always does. Then this book was set to be released in about 3 weeks and I was yet faced with some more adversity. I was informed that because of a malfunction in the online system for my class I had failed one of my final courses. I was sitting at about a 3.9 GPA and was looking to graduate Summa Cum Laude in the weeks to come. However, because of this I was suspended from the program and told I wouldn't be able to graduate. I was devastated and couldn't seem to understand the reasoning. I had been working harder than ever and felt as if the world was crashing down on me. I happened to be listening to Marvin Sapp on Pandora and a TD Jakes sermon came on. The sermon was short only about 6 minutes in length. He spoke about being down and not out, delayed but not denied. I said earlier that I don't believe in coincidences at all. How a sermon came on while listening to Marvin Sapp Pandora for songs is still a mystery to me. Funny thing is if this wouldn't have happened this chapter would have never made the book. So, I took this short sermon and analyzed it and consuming at the pros of my situation. I was set to release this book and my App *Melanoid Exchange* alongside each other. I tried to figure out the reasoning and thought the setback might give me more time to cross my "t's" and dot my "I's". Or perhaps it could've just been a

• • •

faith test to know if I could practice everything I had been preaching in this book.

I reminded myself of the faith files I spoke of earlier and while going over the final edits found myself counseling and educating myself through a book that I had wrote. It had been months since I had written the book, this had been a very busy time in my life so many of the concepts had slipped my mind. I was reminded that just because I had been knocked down I was not knocked out. In life things sometimes come out of the woodworks to knock you down but essentially, they knock you up. The setback was indeed a faith test. In the coming days I would find out if I could truly walk it how I talked it. I was reinstated back into the program, cleared to graduate, and was in an even better situation than I was to begin with. I was able to get my grade changed and given extra time to complete the work.

* * *

This is what allowed me to get the app exactly where I needed it to be for the scheduled release date. Faith is indeed a growing muscle. I'm nowhere near where I want to be, but the progression of my faith has helped me drastically in becoming the Hood Scholar. I look at every test as a chance to perfect my craft. Down but not out, delayed but not denied!

Chapter 38

A hood scholar gone to soon

Hebert Johnson 1/2/95 – 1/15/2018

My childhood friend. A fellow hood scholar. Of all my friends he probably had the most in common with me. A man who had the street smarts and also the book smarts. To be honest, after he graduated in December 2017, he motivated me to do the same. My life was kind of in shambles at this time but seeing my fellow friend graduate pushed me to stay on the right path. An honors student, an entrepreneur, and a true hustler. He was gunned down in cold blood, and all I ask is why? Dreams of being the next to make it out of the Hood. He had a vision like no other and not only

talked the talk but he walked the walk.
Herbert Johnson graduated from Bethune
Cookman University in December 2017. He
celebrated a birthday two weeks later. Then
about two weeks after that he was murdered
in cold blood. This is a story that all too
familiar in my hood. The thing that I can't
seem to understand is why take someone out
who has made it out. It's hard enough to
make it out of Broward County, and after
making it to college graduation just to have
your life taken by someone who doesn't
even value his own life is senseless. We
then again have revisited the hate word.
Taking an innocent man's life for no reason
is something I can't seem to get over. I have
come to an understanding that he is in a
better place, but we must do better as a
community. This is normal, and time after
time, almost every day, you can turn on the

● ● ●
235

news and find a black man shot and killed. Where does this stop? We argue and fight for the black lives matter movement. Does a black life really matter? How can we expect our lives to matter to another race when we don't value ourselves? This is just one instance, but there are too many to name. When the white man kills one of us, we want to protest and raise all of this commotion. But when one of our own dies we quickly buy a rest in peace shirt and look to celebrate their life by going to the club. I can recall when someone died in my neighborhood by getting shot at the club. They then went on to have a rest in peace party for him at the same club he was killed at. It has gotten to the point where I have been feeling like who's next. If people were doing things deserving to be shot and killed, then I could understand, but these people are really innocent. But no one cares and we can't expect for anyone to care when we look at it as everyday life. I never have seen anybody make it out of the streets. You either will end up dead or in jail. That's something everyone would hear daily but then when it becomes a reality is when it starts to get scary. It never hits home until it's your sibling, your cousin, or your childhood friend. We like to have our opinions, but we are responsible for killing off our own race.

We are killing off ourselves. Sometimes I look at our issues as a race and face the fact that we just have to do better. Together this can be changed, and I believe we just have to take action. There are a lot of Hood scholars, and I want to see them become all they can be. I feel extremely blessed and feel as if every black man should have the same opportunity. Losing a life at a young age is always a hard thing because you begin to imagine what that child could have become. I was not the first Hood scholar, and most definitely won't be the last. As a race, we must embrace the black youth and show them that they can overcome all of the adversity and become something great. Entertainment and sports are cool, but we have many more talents. There are too many ways to make it to the top. My sole purpose in life I believe, is to encourage the next generation to believe somehow some way that they too make it out of the hood to become a hood scholar.

(Jovante Ham and Herbert Johnson (Left) at signing
day
ceremony 2013 at Plantation High School.)

After word

You now have the blueprint of a hood scholar. The statistics have written us off and said that we would end up dead or in jail. No matter your area of expertise, I hope this book has led you to excel in it despite your upbringings. We have been written off to almost all the finer things in life, and we can't be ok with it. I encourage every boy, girl, woman, or man to embrace the hood and use it to your advantages. We have seen things and overcame things which an individual outside our neighborhood would know nothing about. And when you make it don't be afraid to shout out and give back to where you come from. The younger generation needs us to show them the way. Think of how much easier it may have been for you if you had a positive influence in your corner showing you the way. I challenge everyone reading this text to go back to your old neighborhood and mentor someone who reminds you of yourself. I guarantee you it won't be a hard task. Fact of the matter is they need us. Hood scholars are rare and it's because we lack the knowledge of how to become one. Get out and mold the next Hood Scholar!

About the Author

Jovante Ham is a young professional hauling from Fort Lauderdale, Florida. Ham is an avid believer in the Lord and savior Jesus Christ. He resides in Fort Worth, TX where he works as an Aerospace Hardware engineer for Lockheed Martin Aeronautics. He has a Bachelor of Science degree in Computer Engineering from Prairie View A&M University where he lettered in football 4 years. He also holds a Master of Engineering Management from Arkansas State University. Ham is the CEO of Melanoid Exchange LLC which feature his app *Melanoid Exchange*. He loves and devotes his time to his daughter Journey Lee Ham, fiancé Darsha Carter, and family and friends.

Made in the USA
Coppell, TX
14 November 2020

41382954R00141